"When I was a much younger and more optimistic writer, I found myself believing that the writing of a poem, alone, could change the circumstances of an immensely flawed world, no matter what the poem was (or wasn't) asking, no matter what it was (or wasn't) doing. A part of my re-education was finding the poetry of Diane di Prima, specifically these *Revolutionary Letters*. Poems that are indictments, of not only the speaker, but also the reader. Poems that allow for rage and dissatisfaction to be channeled outward into something beyond the page. There is a generosity and affection in these poems that I find myself returning to, always, when I'm at my most cynical and feeling lost for any understanding of what a better world might look like. When I need to be grounded and re-centered in my understanding of community care as a living, breathing, full-time mission. And, quite simply, when I need to be reminded of how language can begin on the page, and echo far beyond."

—Hanif Abdurraqib

"The bourgeois poet says poetry makes nothing happen, but what's astonishing about Diane di Prima's *Revolutionary Letters* is how these poems are adamantly useful. A manual of insurgent instruction, these poems tell you how to mitigate tear gas and sleep deprivation, eat a healthy diet, and overthrow the state. Less interested in displaying lyric interiority than inculcating a radical ideology, di Prima's letters are explosive and nourishing—and that most paradoxical thing, a classic text from an antisystemic tradition. Not simply a relic from a New Left past, this book is ever more urgent in our moment, as a resurgent left faces down the apocalypse. *Revolutionary Letters* is a time machine towards a better future."

—Ken Chen

"With this new and expanded edition we are offered a window onto a master poet redefining revolution over her lifetime (through a prism). Di Prima continues to interrogate the ways in which we have been taught to live, love, eat, write, fight and take control. In her classic poem 'Rant' ('Revolutionary Letter #75') she describes this mindset as 'a multidimensional chess / which is divination / & strategy'. This time reading through I was reminded of Baraka's *Wise, Why's, Y's* and Ginsberg's *The Fall of America*. How can we make the most of this book and its wisdom? It's not enough to simply read it or even to write our own *Revolutionary Letters*. These poems are not realized until we are called upon to act."

—Cedar Sigo

"How do 'we' keep fighting? There is no one way, but sometimes you think about lines in Diane di Prima's *Revolutionary Letters*. Di Prima's 'letters' feel like they were written to the all of you that always is somewhere coming together. They remind you that you are a part of something, that as sure as you have enemies who want things like jobs, you have friends who want everything. The new letters in this expanded edition continue di Prima's tradition of telling you things you need to know—like 'you have only / so much / ammunition' & how a poem can matter as 'the memory / of the poem / tak[es] root in / thousands / of minds.' & here you thought this classic couldn't get any better."

—Wendy Trevino

"*Revolutionary Letters* is a practical guide to visionary living, a necessary handbook for all who fight for the end of prisons, borders, and environmental degradation. Its poems mourn, conspire, and command, by turns sensuous, brisk, and searing. Di Prima challenges us endlessly to be equal to our own bodies, to the body of the earth: 'sense and sex are boundless, & the call / is to be boundless with them.' I turn to this book when I am depleted by the news, because di Prima's voice is heartening, an offering of strength."

—Sophia Dahlin

REVOLUTIONARY LETTERS

50th Anniversary Edition

Diane di Prima

City Lights Books | San Francisco

The Pocket Poets Series : Number 27

Library of Congress Cataloging-in-Publication Data

Names: Di Prima, Diane, author.
Title: Revolutionary letters / Diane di Prima.
Description: Expanded edition. | San Francisco : City Lights Books, 2021. |
  Series: Pocket poets series ; No. 27
Identifiers: LCCN 2021008208 | ISBN 9780872868793 (hardback)
Subjects: LCGFT: Poetry.
Classification: LCC PS3507.I68 R4 2021 | DDC 811/.54—dc23
LC record available at https://lccn.loc.gov/2021008208

Cover calligraphy by Lawrence Ferlinghetti.

Thank you to Sara Larsen for her assistance.
City Lights also thanks Mary Catherine Kinniburgh for research on previous
editions.

City Lights Books are published at the City Lights Bookstore
261 Columbus Avenue, San Francisco, CA 94133
www.citylights.com

just under the scorched earth
under the skin of the old

itta come, sisters!

The *REVOLUTIONARY LETTERS*
are dedicated to Bob Dylan;
and to my grandfather, Domenico Mallozzi,
friend of the great anarchist dreamers of his time,
who read me Dante at the age of four
and named my mother after Emma Goldman.

APRIL FOOL BIRTHDAY POEM FOR GRANDPA

Today is your
birthday and I have tried
writing these things before
but now
in the gathering madness, I want to
thank you
for telling me what to expect
for pulling
no punches,   back there in that scrubbed Bronx parlor
thank you
for honestly weeping in time to
innumerable heartbreaking
Italian operas for
pulling my hair when I
pulled the leaves off the trees so I'd
know how it feels, we are
involved in it now, revolution, up to our
knees and the tide is rising, I embrace
strangers on the street, filled with their love and
mine, the love you told us had to come or we
die, told them all in that Bronx park, me listening in
spring Bronx dusk, breathing stars, so glorious
to me your white hair, your height your fierce
blue eyes, rare among Italians, I stood
a ways off looking up at you, my grandpa
people listened to, I stand
a ways off listening as I pour out soup
young men with light in their faces
at my table, talking love, talking revolution
which *is* love, spelled backwards, how
you would love us all, would thunder your anarchist wisdom

at us, would thunder Dante, and Giordano Bruno, orderly men
bent to your ends, well I want you to know
we do it for you, and your ilk, for Carlo Tresca
for Sacco and Vanzetti, without knowing
it, or thinking about it, as we do it for Aubrey Beardsley
Oscar Wilde (all street lights
shall be purple), do it
for Trotsky and Shelley and big/dumb
Kropotkin
Eisenstein's *Strike* people, Jean Cocteau's ennui, we do it for
the stars over the Bronx
that they may look on earth
and not be ashamed.

REVOLUTIONARY LETTER #1

I have just realized that the stakes are myself
I have no other
ransom money, nothing to break or barter but my life
my spirit measured out, in bits, spread over
the roulette table, I recoup what I can
nothing else to shove under the nose of the *maître de jeu*
nothing to thrust out the window, no white flag
this flesh all I have to offer, to make the play with
this immediate head, what it comes up with, my move
as we slither over this go board, stepping always
(we hope) between the lines

REVOLUTIONARY LETTER #2

The value of an individual life a credo they taught us
to instill fear, and inaction, "you only live once"
a fog in our eyes, we are
endless as the sea, not separate, we die
a million times a day, we are born
a million times, each breath life and death:
get up, put on your shoes, get
started, someone will finish

Tribe
an organism, one flesh, breathing joy as the stars
breathe destiny down on us, get
going, join hands, see to business, thousands of sons
will see to it when you fall, you will grow
a thousand times in the bellies of your sisters

REVOLUTIONARY LETTER #3

store water; make a point of filling your bathtub
at the first news of trouble: they turned off the water
in the 4th ward for a whole day during the Newark riots;
or better yet make a habit
of keeping the tub clean and full when not in use
change this once a day, it should be good enough
for washing, flushing toilets when necessary
and cooking, in a pinch, but it's a good idea
to keep some bottled water handy too
get a couple of five gallon jugs and keep them full
for cooking

store food—dry stuff like rice and beans stores best
goes farthest. SALT VERY IMPORTANT: it's health and energy
healing too, keep a couple pounds
sea salt around, and, because we're spoiled, some tins
tuna, etc. to keep up morale—keep up the sense
of "balanced diet" "protein intake" remember
the stores may be closed for quite some time, the trucks
may not enter your section of the city for weeks
you can cool it indefinitely

with 20 lb brown rice
        20 lb whole wheat flour
        10 lb cornmeal
        10 lb good beans—kidney or soy
          5 lb sea salt
          2 qts good oil

dried fruit and nuts
add nutrients and a sense of luxury
to this diet, a squash or coconut
in a cool place in your pad will keep six months

remember we are all used to eating less
than the "average American" and take it easy
before we
ever notice we're hungry the rest of the folk will be starving
used as they are to meat and fresh milk daily
and help will arrive, until the day no help arrives
and then you're on your own.

hoard matches, we aren't good
at rubbing sticks together any more
a tinder box is useful, if you can work it
don't count on gas stove, gas heater
electric light
keep hibachi and charcoal, CHARCOAL STARTER a help
kerosene lamp and candles, learn to keep warm
with breathing
remember the blessed American habit of bundling

REVOLUTIONARY LETTER #4

Left to themselves people
grow their hair.
Left to themselves they
take off their shoes.
Left to themselves they make love
sleep easily
share blankets, dope & children
they are not lazy or afraid
they plant seeds, they smile, they
speak to one another. The word
coming into its own: touch of love
on the brain, the ear.

We return with the sea, the tides
we return as often as leaves, as numerous
as grass, gentle, insistent, we remember
the way,
our babes toddle barefoot thru the cities of the universe

REVOLUTIONARY LETTER #5

at some point
you may be called upon
to keep going for several days without sleep;
keep some ups around. to be
clearheaded, avoid "comedown" as much as possible,
take vitamin B along with amphetamines, try
powdered guarana root, available
at herb drugstores, it is an up
used by Peruvian mountainfolk, tastes
like mocha (bitter) can be put in tea
will clear your head, increase oxygen supply
keep you going past amphetamine wooziness

at some point
you may have to crash, under tension, keep some downs
on hand, you may have to cool out
sickness, or freak-out, or sorrow, keep some downs
on hand, I don't mean
tranquilizers, ye olde fashioned SLEEPING PILL
(sleep heals heads, heals souls) chloral hydrate
(Mickey Finn) one of the best, but
nembutal, etc. OK in a pinch, remember
no liquor with barbiturates

at some point
you will need painkillers, darvon
is glorified shit, stash some codeine & remember
it's about five times more effective
if taken with aspirin

ups, downs & painkillers are
the essence: antibiotics
for extreme infections, any good
wide-spectrum one will do, avoid penicillin
too many allergies, speaking of which
cortisone is good for really bad attacks
(someone who freaks out asthma-style, or with hives)

USE ALL THESE AS LITTLE
as possible, side effects multifarious
and they cloud the brain
tend to weaken the body and obscure
judgment

ginseng tea, ginger compresses, sea salt,
prayer and love
are better healers, easier come by, save the others
for life and death trips, you will know
when you see one

REVOLUTIONARY LETTER #6

avoid the folk
who find *Bonnie and Clyde* too violent
who see the blood but not the energy form
they love us and want us to practice birth control
they love us and want the Hindus to kill their cows
they love us and have a colorless tasteless powder
        which is the perfect synthetic food …

REVOLUTIONARY LETTER #7

there are those who can tell you
how to make molotov cocktails, flamethrowers,
bombs whatever
you might be needing
find them and learn, define
your aim clearly, choose your ammo
with that in mind

it is not a good idea to tote a gun
or knife
unless you are proficient in its use
all swords are two-edged, can be used against you
by anyone who can get 'em away from you

it is
possible even on the east coast
to find an isolated place for target practice
success
will depend mostly on your state of mind:
meditate, pray, make love, be prepared
at any time, to die

but don't get uptight: the guns
will not win this one, they are
an incidental part of the action
which we better damn well be good at
what will win
is mantras, the sustenance we give each other,
the energy we plug into
      (the fact that we touch
        share food)
the buddha nature
of everyone, friend and foe, like a million earthworms
tunneling under this structure
till it falls

REVOLUTIONARY LETTER #8

Everytime you pick the spot for a be-in
a demonstration, a march, a rally, you are choosing the ground
for a potential battle.
You are still calling these shots.
Pick your terrain with that in mind.
Remember the old gang rules:
stick to your neighborhood, don't let them lure you
to Central Park everytime, I would hate
to stumble bloody out of that park to find help:
Central Park West or Fifth Avenue, which would you
choose?

go to love-ins
with incense, flowers, food, and a plastic bag
with a damp cloth in it, for tear gas, wear no jewelry
wear clothes you can move in easily, wear no glasses
contact lenses
earrings for pierced ears are especially hazardous

try to be clear
in front, what you will do if it comes
to trouble
if you're going to try to split stay out of the center
don't stampede or panic others
don't waver between active and passive resistance
know your limitations, bear contempt
neither for yourself, nor any of your brothers

NO ONE WAY WORKS, it will take all of us
shoving at the thing from all sides
to bring it down.

REVOLUTIONARY LETTER #9

advocating
the overthrow of government is a crime
overthrowing it is something else
altogether. it is sometimes called
revolution
but don't kid yourself: government
is not where it's at: it's only
a good place to start:
      1. kill head of Dow Chemical
      2. destroy plant
      3. MAKE IT UNPROFITABLE FOR THEM
to build again.
i.e., destroy the concept of money
as we know it, get rid of interest,
savings, inheritance
(Pound's money, as dated coupons that come in the mail
to everyone, and are void in 30 days
is still a good idea)
or, let's start with no money at all and invent it
    if we need it
or, mimeograph it and everyone
    print as much as they want
    and see what happens

declare a moratorium on debt
the Continental Congress did
"on all debts public and private"

& no one "owns" the land
it can be held
for use, no man holding more
than he can work, himself and family working

let no one work for another
except for love, and what you make
above your needs be given to the tribe
a Common-Wealth

None of us knows the answers, think about
these things.
The day will come when we will have to know
the answers.

REVOLUTIONARY LETTER #10

These are transitional years and the dues
will be heavy.
Change is quick but revolution
will take a while.
America has not even begun as yet.
This continent is seed.

REVOLUTIONARY LETTER #11

drove across
San Joaquin Valley
with Kirby Doyle
grooving
getting free Digger meat
for Free City Convention
grooving
behind talk of Kirby's family
been here a long time
grooving
friendship renewed, neat pickup truck, we stopped
at a gas station
man uptight at the
sight of us, sight of Kirby's hair, his friendly
loose face, my hair, our dress
man surly, uptight, we drove
away brought down
(across fields of insecticide and migrant workers)
and
"Man" I said "that cat
so uptight, what's he
so uptight about, it's not
your hair, not really, it's just
what the TV tells him about hippies
got him scared, what he reads in
his magazines
got him scared, we got to
come out from behind the image
sit down with him, if he

sat down to a beer with you he'd find
a helluva lot more to say than he'll find
with the man who makes your image
he's got nothing in common
with the men who run his mind, who tell him
what to think of us"

SMASH THE MEDIA, I said,
AND BURN THE SCHOOLS
so people can meet, can sit
and talk to each other, warm and close
no TV image flickering
between them.

REVOLUTIONARY LETTER #12

the vortex of creation is the vortex of destruction
the vortex of artistic creation is the vortex of self destruction
the vortex of political creation is the vortex of flesh destruction
    flesh is in the fire, it curls and terribly warps
    fat is in the fire, it drips and sizzling sings
    bones are in the fire
       they crack tellingly in
       subtle hieroglyphs of oracle
    charcoal singed
    the smell of your burning hair
for every revolutionary must at last will his own destruction
rooted as he is in the past he sets out to destroy

REVOLUTIONARY LETTER #13

now let me tell you
what is a Brahmasastra
Brahmasastra, hindu weapon of war
near as I can make out
a flying wedge of mind energy
hurled at the foe   by god or hero
or many heroes
hurled at a problem or enemy
cracking it

Brahmasastra can be made
by any or all
can be made by all of us
straight or tripping, thinking together
like: all of us stop the war
at nine o'clock tomorrow, each take one soldier
see him clearly, love him, take the gun
out of his hand, lead him to a quiet spot
sit him down, sit with him as he takes a joint
of viet cong grass from his pocket . . .

Brahmasastra can be made
by all of us, tripping together
winter solstice
at home, or in park, or wandering
sitting with friends
blinds closed, or on porch, no be-in

no need
to gather publicity
just gather spirit, see the forest growing
put back the big trees
put back the buffalo
the grasslands of the midwest with their herds
        of elk and deer
put fish in clean Great Lakes
desire that all surface water on the planet
be clean again. Kneel down and drink
from whatever brook or lake you conjure up.

REVOLUTIONARY LETTER #14

are you prepared
to hide someone in your home indefinitely
say, two to six weeks, you going out
for food, etc., so he never
hits the street, to keep your friends away
coolly, so they ask no questions, to nurse
him or her, as necessary, to know
"first aid" and healing (not to freak out
at the sight of torn or half-cooked flesh)
to pass him on at the right time to the next
station, to cross the canadian border, with a child
so that the three of you
look like one family, no questions asked
or fewer, to stash letters, guns, or bombs
forget about them
till they are called for, to KEEP YOUR MOUTH SHUT
not to "trust"
even your truelove, that is,
lay no more knowledge on him than he needs
to do his part of it, a kindness
we all must extend to each other in this game

REVOLUTIONARY LETTER #15

When you seize Columbia, when you
seize Paris, take
the media, tell the people what you're doing
what you're up to and why and how you mean
to do it, how they can help, keep the news
coming, steady, you have 70 years
of media conditioning to combat, it is a wall
you must get through, somehow, to reach
the instinctive man, who is struggling like a plant
for light, for air

when you seize a town, a campus, get hold of the power
stations, the water, the transportation,
forget to negotiate, forget how
to negotiate, don't wait for De Gaulle or Kirk
to abdicate, they won't, you are not
"demonstrating" you are fighting
a war, fight to win, don't wait for Johnson or
Humphrey or Rockefeller, to agree to your terms
take what you need, "it's free
because it's yours"

REVOLUTIONARY LETTER #16

we are eating up the planet, the *New York Times*
takes a forest every Sunday, Los Angeles
draws its water from the Sacramento Valley
the rivers of British Columbia are ours
on lease for 99 years

every large factory is an infringement
of our god-given right to light and air
to clean and flowing rivers stocked with fish
to the very possibility of life
for our children's children, we will have to
look carefully, i.e., do we really want/
need
electricity and at what cost in natural resource
human resource
do we need cars, when petroleum
pumped from the earth poisons the land around
for 100 years, pumped from the car
poisons the hard-pressed cities, or try this
statistic, the USA
has 5% of the world's people uses over
50% of the world's goods, our garbage
holds matter for survival for uncounted
"underdeveloped" nations

REVOLUTIONARY LETTER #17

we will all feel the pinch
there will *not* be
a cadillac and a 40,000 dollar home
for everyone
simply
the planet will not bear it.

What there will be is enough
food, enough
of the "necessities", luxuries
will have to go by the board

even the poorest of us
will have to give up something
to live free

REVOLUTIONARY LETTER #18

let's talk about splitting, splitting is an art
frequently called upon in revolution
retreat, says the *I Ching*, must not be confused
with flight, and furthermore, frequently it furthers
ONE TO HAVE SOMEWHERE TO GO

i.e., know in advance
the person/place you can go to
means to get there
keep money (cash) in house for travelling
an extra set of i.d., Robert Williams
was warned by his own TV set when the Man
was coming for him,
he had his loot at home, his wife and kids
all crossed the country with him, into CANADA
and on to CUBA

it's a good idea
to have good, working transportation "wheels", one friend
has two weeks stashed in his vw bus
food, water, matches, clothing, blankets, gas, he can go
at least that long, before he hits a town, can leave
at any time
something to think about . . .

REVOLUTIONARY LETTER #19
FOR THE POOR PEOPLE'S CAMPAIGN

if what you want is jobs
for everyone, you are still the enemy,
you have not thought thru, clearly
what that means

if what you want is housing,
industry
          (GE on the Navaho
          reservation)
a car for everyone, garage, refrigerator,
TV, more plumbing, scientific
freeways, you are still
the enemy, you have chosen
to sacrifice the planet for a few years of some
science fiction utopia, if what you want

still is, or can be, schools
where all our kids are pushed into one shape, are taught
it's better to be "American" than Black
or Indian, or Jap, or PR, where Dick
and Jane become and are the dream, do *you*
look like Dick's father, don't you think your kid
secretly wishes you did

if what you want
is clinics where the AMA
can feed you pills to keep you weak, or sterile
shoot germs into your kids, while Merck & Co
grows richer
if you want
free psychiatric help for everyone
so that the shrinks
pimps for this decadence, can make
it flower for us, if you want
if you still want a piece
a small piece of suburbia, green lawn
laid down by the square foot
color TV, whose radiant energy
kills brain cells, whose subliminal ads
brainwash your children, have taken over
your dreams

degrees from universities which are nothing
more than slum landlords, festering sinks
of lies, so you too can go forth
and lie to others on some greeny campus

THEN YOU ARE STILL
THE ENEMY, you are selling
yourself short, remember
you can have what you ask for, ask for
everything

REVOLUTIONARY LETTER #20
for Huey Newton

I will not rest
till we walk free & fearless on the earth
each doing in the manner of his blood
& tribe, peaceful in the free air

till all can seek, unhindered
the shape of their thought
no black cloud fear or guilt
between them & the sun, no babies burning
young men locked away, no paper world
to come between flesh & flesh in human
encounter

till the young women
come into their own, honored & fearless
birthing strong babes
loving & dancing

till we can at last
lose some of our sternness, return
to our own thoughts, till laughter
bounces off our hills & fills
our plains

REVOLUTIONARY LETTER #21

Can you
own land, can you
own house, own rights
to other's labor, (stocks or factories
or money, loaned at interest)
what about
the yield of same, crops, autos
airplanes dropping bombs, can you
own real estate, so others
pay you rent? to whom
does the water belong, to whom
will the air belong, as it gets rarer?
the american indians say that a man
can own no more than he can carry away
on his horse.

REVOLUTIONARY LETTER #22

what do you want
your kids to learn, do you care
if they know factoring, chemical formulae, theory
of numbers, equations, philosophy, semantics
symbolic logic, latin, history, socalled, which is
merely history of mind of western man, least interesting
of numberless manifestations on this planet?

do you care
if he learns to eat off the woods, to set
a broken arm, to mend
his own clothes, cook simple food, deliver
a calf or baby? if there are cars should he not
be able to keep his running?
how will he learn these things, will he learn them
cut off in a plaster box, encased
in a larger cement box called "school" dealing with paper
from morning till night, grinding no clay or mortar, no
pigment, setting no seedlings in black earth
come spring, how will he
know to trap a rabbit, build a raft
to navigate by stars, or find safe ground
to sleep on? what is he doing all his learning years
inside, as if the planet were no more than a vehicle
for carrying our plastic constructs around the sun

REVOLUTIONARY LETTER #23

a lack of faith is simply a lack of courage
one who says "I wish I could believe that" means simply that he
is coward, is pleased
to be spectator, on this scene where there are no spectators
where all hands not actually working are working against
as they lie idle, folded in lap, or holding up newspapers
full of lies, or wrapped around steering wheel, on one more
pleasure trip

REVOLUTIONARY LETTER #24

Have you thought about the American aborigines
who will inhabit
this continent? Cave dwellers, tent people, tree dwellers, will your
great-grandchildren be among them? Will they sell
artifacts—abalone or wool—to the affluent
highly civilized Africans
who come here in the summer, will they wear
buckskin, or cotton, loincloth, run down
deer, catch fish barehanded, build teepees, hogans, remember
to use the wheel, to write, to speak
or simply drum & pipe, smiling, will your
great-grandchildren be among them?

REVOLUTIONARY LETTER #25

Know every way
out of your house, where it goes, every alley
on the block, which back yards connect, which walls
are scalable, which bushes
will hold a man.
Construct at least one man-sized hiding place
in your walls, know for sure which neighbors
will let you sneak in the back door & saunter out the front
while the Man is parked in your driveway, or tearing
your pad apart, which neighbors won't be home, which cellar doors
are open—whom you can summon in your neighborhood
to do your errands, check the block, set up
a getaway while you sit tight inside & your house
is watched . . .

REVOLUTIONARY LETTER #26

"DOES THE END
JUSTIFY THE MEANS?" this is
process, there is no end, there are only
means, each one
had better justify itself.
To whom?

REVOLUTIONARY LETTER #27

How much
can we afford to lose, before we win, can we
cut hair, or give up drugs, take
job, join Minute Men, marry, wear their clothes
play bingo, what
can we stomach, how soon
does it leave its mark, can we
living straight in a straight part of town still see
our people, can we live
if we don't see our people? "It is better
to lose & win, than win & be
defeated" sd Gertrude Stein, which wd you
choose?

REVOLUTIONARY LETTER #28

O my brothers
busted for pot, for looting, for loving
young beautiful brothers & sisters, for holding out hope
in both hands to the Man, enraging him
O my sisters, freaking out this moment
      this beautiful summer evening
in all the cages of America
while the sun goes down on this fabled & holy land:

know that we have this land, we are filling its crevices
its caves and forests, its coastlines and holy places
with our mating flesh, with the fierce play of our children
      our numbers increasing
we are approaching your cells, to cut you loose
to march triumphant with you, crying out
to Maitreya, across the Pacific

REVOLUTIONARY LETTER #29

beware of those
who say we are the beautiful losers
who stand in their long hair and wait to be punished
who weep on beaches for our isolation

we are not alone: we have brothers in all the hills
we have sisters in the jungles and in the ozarks
we even have brothers on the frozen tundra
they sit by their fires, they sing, they gather arms
they multiply: they will reclaim the earth

nowhere we can go but they are waiting for us
no exile where we will not hear welcome home
"good morning brother, let me work with you
good morning sister, let me
fight by your side"

REVOLUTIONARY LETTER #30
to Those Who Sold the Revolution Summer of '68

remember to wear a hat, if you have a hat
and stick your hair inside it, if it's long hair
or don't, wear shoes if it's snowing and you have shoes
remember they buyout all the leaders, be a leader
if you want to be bought out, but remember to
tell the truth, just before they buy you, tell the truth
loud, and the kids will hear you, not hear your money
as it falls on the liquorstore counter, day after day
not hear your dreams of nightmare betrayal and torture
not hear your mercedes, they'll hear the truth you spoke
they'll believe you and honor you after you die, brought down
by that cia bullet you can't avoid just by taking their money
they'll believe you and DO WHAT YOU SAY
NOT WHAT YOU DO

REVOLUTIONARY LETTER #31
for LeRoi, at long last

not all the works of Mozart worth one human life
not all the brocades of the Potala palace
better we should wear homespun, than some in orlon
some in Thailand silk
the children of Bengal weave gold thread in silk saris
six years old, eight years old, for export, they don't sing
the singers are for export, Folkways records
better we should all have homemade flutes
and practice excruciatingly upon them, one hundred years
till we learn to
make our own music

REVOLUTIONARY LETTER #32

not western civilization, but civilization itself
is the disease which is eating us
not the last five thousand years, but the last twenty thousand
are the cancer
not modern cities, but the city, not
capitalism, but ism, art, religion, once they are
separate enough to be seen and named, named art named
religion, once they are not
simply the daily acts of life which bring the rain, bring bread
heal, bring

the herds close enough to hunt, birth the children
simply the acts of song, the acts of power, now lost
to us these many years, not killing a few white men will bring
back power, not killing all the white men, but killing
the white man in each of us, killing the desire
for brocade, for gold, for champagne brandy, which sends
people out of the sun and out of their lives to create
COMMODITY for our pleasure, what claim
do we have, can we make, on another's time, another's
life blood, show me
a city which does not consume the air and water
for miles around it, Mohenjo-daro was a blot
on the village culture of India, the cities of Egypt sucked
the life of millions, show me
an artifact of city which has the power
as flesh has power, as spirit of man
has power

REVOLUTIONARY LETTER #33

how far back
are we willing to go? that seems to be
the question. the more we give up
the more we will be blessed, the more
we give up, the further back we go, can we
make it under the sky again, in moving tribes
that settle, build, move on and build again
owning only what we carry, do we need
the village, division of labor, a friendly potlatch
a couple of times a year, or must it be
merely a "cybernetic civilization"
which may or may not save the water, but will not
show us our root, or our original face, return
us to the source, how far
(forward is back) are we willing to go
after all?

REVOLUTIONARY LETTER #34

hey man let's make a revolution, let's give
every man a thunderbird
color TV, a refrigerator, free
antibiotics, let's build
apartments with a separate bedroom for every child
inflatable plastic sofas, vitamin pills
with all our daily requirements that come in the mail
free gas & electric & telephone &
no rent. why not?

hey man, let's make a revolution, let's
turn off the power, turn on the
stars at night, put metal
back in the earth, or at least not take it out
anymore, make lots of guitars and flutes, teach the chicks
how to heal with herbs, let's learn
to live with each other in a smaller space, and build
hogans, and domes and teepees all over the place
BLOW UP THE PETROLEUM LINES, make the cars
into flower pots or sculptures or live
in the bigger ones, why not?

REVOLUTIONARY LETTER #35

rise up, my
brothers, do not
bow your heads any longer, or pray
except to the spirit you waken, the
spirit you bring to birth, it
never was on earth, rise up, do not
droop, smoking hash or opium, dreaming sweetness, perhaps
there will be time for that, on the long beaches
lying in love with the few of us who are left, but now
the earth cries out for aid, our brothers
and sisters set aside their childhoods, prepare
to fight, what choice have we but join them, in their hands
rests the survival of the very planet, the health
of the solar system, for we are one
with the stars, and the spirit we forge
they wait for, Christ, Buddha, Krishna
Paracelsus, had but a taste, we must reclaim
the planet, re-occupy
this ground
the peace we seek was never seen before, the earth
BELONGS, at last, TO THE LIVING

REVOLUTIONARY LETTER #36

who is the we, who is
the they in this thing, did
we or they kill the indians, not me
my people brought here, cheap labor to exploit
a continent for them, did we
or they exploit it? do you
admit complicity, say "*we*
have to get out of Vietnam, *we* really should
stop poisoning the water, etc." look closer, look again
secede, declare your independence, don't accept
a share of the guilt *they* want to lay on *us*
MAN IS INNOCENT & BEAUTIFUL & born
to perfect bliss they envy, heavy deeds
make heavy hearts and to *them*
life is suffering.   stand clear.

REVOLUTIONARY LETTER #37

GEOGRAPHY, U.S.A.

the east edge is
megalopolis, is
Washington, DC, spread out
800 miles, ecology
totally fucked up, even
the brothers there do not completely believe
that they can win; the west edge
is languorous w/ wealth, there venison
is brought down from the hills & figs & wine
from abandoned orchards, the sisters
raise their bastard young on welfare checks & rotten
sprayed vegetables, talk "free", talk end of money, for them
the war is over, all the wars; the middle
is hardly heard from yet, it is
stirring, stretching muscles, bare bones of continent, eternal
progression of young barbarians
huge boiling meat-fed hordes who can't be taught
there's anything to lose, angelic herds whose unholy yell
is gonna shake us all

REVOLUTIONARY LETTER #38

NOT PEOPLE'S PARK
PEOPLE'S PLANET, CAN THEY
FENCE THAT ONE IN, BULLDOZE IT
4 A.M.?

REVOLUTIONARY LETTER #39

let me tell you, sisters, that on May 30th I went to one of our
life festivals
dropped acid in Tompkins Square Park with my
brothers & sisters
danced in the sun, till the stars
came out & the pigs
drove around us in a circle, where we stood
touching each other & loving, then I
went home & made love like a flower, like two flowers opening
to each other, we were
the jewel in the lotus, next morning still high wandered uptown
to Natural History Museum & there
in a room of Peruvian fauna, birds
of paradise I saw as a past, like the dinosaurs
saw birds pass from the earth &
flowers, most trees & small creatures:
chipmunks & rabbits & squirrels & delicate wildflowers
saw the earth bare & smooth, austerely plastic & efficient
men feeding hydroponically, working like ants
thought flatly, without regret (I have unlearned
regret)
>   "WHAT BEAUTIFUL CREATURES
>   USED TO LIVE ON THE EARTH"

REVOLUTIONARY LETTER #40
   for Emmet Grogan

if the power of the word is anything, America
your oil fields burning
your cities in ruins, smoldering, pillaged by children
your cars broken down, at a standstill, choking the roads
your citizens standing beside them, bewildered, or choosing
a packload of objects (what they can carry away) if the
power of the word lives, America, your power lines down
eagle-eyed lines of electric, of telephone
towers of radio transmission
toppled & rankling in the fields, setting the hay ablaze
your newspapers useless, your populace illiterate
wiping their asses with them
IF THE WORD HAS POWER YOU SHALL NOT STAND
AMERICA, the wilderness is spreading from the parks
you have fenced it into, already
desert blows through Las Vegas, the sea licks its chops
at the oily edges of Los Angeles
the camels are breeding, the bears, the elk are increasing
so are the indians and the very poor
do you stir in your sleep, America, do you dream of your power
pastel colored oil tanks from sea to shining sea?
sleep well, America, we stand by your bedside
the word has power, the chant is going up

REVOLUTIONARY LETTER #41

Revolution: a turning, as the earth
turns, among planets, as the sun
turns round some (darker) star, the galaxy
describes a yin-yang spiral in the aether, we turn
from dark to light, turn
faces of pain & fear, the dawn
awash among them

REVOLUTIONARY LETTER #42

what is this
"overpopulation" problem, have you
looked at it, clearly, do you know

ten times as much land needed if we eat
hamburger, instead of grain, we can
all fit, not hungry, if we minimize
our needs, RIP OFF LARGE EMPTY RANCHES, make the food
nutritious: chemical fertilizers
have to go, nitrates
poison the water, large scale machine farming
has to go, the soil
is blowing away (300 years
to make one inch of topsoil), do you know

40% of the women of Puerto Rico
already sterilized, transistor radios
the "sterilization bonus" in India, all propaganda
aimed at the "non-white" and "poor white" populations

something like 90% of the land of USA
belongs to 5% of the population
how can they hold on
when the hordes of the infants of the very poor
grow up, grow strong

REVOLUTIONARY LETTER #43

the map: first goal is *health*
strong bodies make strong spirit, Venceremos Brigade
coming back from Cuba discover they know how to breathe
they can get up with the sun, first thing
to zap the sugar habit, get rid of meat
& heavy drugs, to eat no chemicals, no processed food
first step:
to find out what health feels like, even keel
tireless energy pouring steady through

then, prana (vital energy) moving smooth
thru all yr flesh: next goal release
sexual force—strong flesh becomes bright flesh
anger becomes "Buddha's anger" a steady roar
righteous, behind yr action, not spasmodic, threatens
no self-destruction, loose touch on
brothers & sisters, loose force (& contain it)
Holy Power
to build up, or pull down

REVOLUTIONARY LETTER #44
for my sisters

As we know that blood
is birth, agony
breaks open doors, as we
can bend, graciously, beneath burdens, undermine
like rain, or earthworms, as our cries
yield to the cries of the newborn, as we hear
the plea in the voices around us, not words
of passion or cunning, discount
anger or pride, grow strong
in our own strength, women's alchemy, quick arms
to pull down walls, we liberate
out of our knowledge, labor, sucking babes, we
liberate, and nourish, as the earth

REVOLUTIONARY LETTER #45

and it seems to me the struggle has to be waged
on a number of different levels:

they have computers to cast the *I Ching* for them
but we have yarrow stalks
and the stars
it is a battle of energies, of force-fields, what the newspapers
call a battle of ideas

to take hold of the magic any way we can
and use it in total faith
to seek help in realms we have been taught to think of
as "mythological"

to contact ALL LEVELS of one's own being
& loose the forces therein
always seeking in this to remain psychically inconspicuous
on the not so unlikely chance
that those we have thought of as "instigators"
are just the front men for a gang of black magicians
based "somewhere else" in space
to whom the WHOLE of earth is a colony to exploit
(the "Nova Mob" not so far out as you think)

Best not to place bodies in the line of fire
but to seek other means: study the Sioux
learn not to fuck up as they did—another ghost dance
started on Haight Street in 1967
We ain't seen the end of it yet

REVOLUTIONARY LETTER #46

And as you learn the magic, learn to believe it
Don't be "surprised" when it works, you undercut
your power.

REVOLUTIONARY LETTER #47

TO BE FREE we've got to be free of
any idea of freedom.
Today the State Dept lifted the ban on
travel to China, and closed
Merritt College.

REVOLUTIONARY LETTER #48

Be careful.
With what relief do we fall back on
the tale, so often told in revolutions
that *now* we must
organize, obey the rules, so that *later*
we can be free. It is the point
at which the revolution stops. To be carried forward
later & in another country, this is
the pattern, but we can
break the pattern

                   learn now we see
with all our skin, smell with our eyes too
sense & sex are boundless & the call
is to be boundless in them, make the joy
now, that we want, no shape
for space & time now but the shapes we will

REVOLUTIONARY LETTER #49

Free Julian Beck
Free Timothy Leary
Free seven million starving in Pakistan
Free all political prisoners
Free Angela Davis
Free Soledad brothers
Free Martin Sobel
Free Sacco & Vanzetti
Free Big Bill Hayward
Free Sitting Bull
Free Crazy Horse
Free all political prisoners
Free Billy the Kid
Free Jesse James
Free all political prisoners
Free Nathan Hale
Free Joan of Arc
Free Galileo & Bruno & Eckhart
Free Jesus Christ
Free Socrates
Free all political prisoners
Free all political prisoners
All prisoners are political prisoners
Every pot smoker a political prisoner
Every holdup man a political prisoner
Every forger a political prisoner
Every angry kid who smashed a window a political prisoner
Every whore, pimp, murderer, a political prisoner

Every pederast, dealer, drunk driver, burglar
Poacher, striker, strike breaker, rapist
Polar bear at San Francisco zoo, political prisoner
Ancient wise turtle at Detroit Aquarium, political prisoner
Flamingoes dying in Phoenix tourist park, political prisoners
Otters in Tucson Desert Museum, political prisoners
Elk in Wyoming grazing behind barbed wire, political prisoners
Prairie dogs poisoned in New Mexico, war casualties
(Mass grave of Wyoming gold eagles, a battlefield)
Every kid in school a political prisoner
Every lawyer in his cubicle a political prisoner
Every doctor brainwashed by AMA a political prisoner
Every housewife a political prisoner
Every teacher lying thru sad teeth a political prisoner
Every indian on reservation a political prisoner
Every black man a political prisoner
Every faggot hiding in bar a political prisoner
Every junkie shooting up in john a political prisoner
Every woman a political prisoner
Every woman a political prisoner
You are political prisoner locked in tense body
You are political prisoner locked in stiff mind
You are political prisoner locked to your parents
You are political prisoner locked to your past
Free yourself
Free yourself
I am political prisoner locked in anger habit
I am political prisoner locked in greed habit
I am political prisoner locked in fear habit
I am political prisoner locked in dull senses

I am political prisoner locked in numb flesh
Free me
Free me
Help to free me
Free yourself
Help to free me
Free yourself
Help to free me
Free Barry Goldwater
Help to free me
Free Governor Wallace
Free President Nixon
Free J Edgar Hoover
Free them
Free yourself
Free them
Free yourself
Free yourself
Free them
Free yourself
Help to free me
Free us
DANCE

REVOLUTIONARY LETTER #50

Machinery: extended hands of man
doing man's work. Diverted rivers
washing my clothes, diverted fire
dancing in wires, making light
and heat. To see it thus is to see it, even
diverted rivers must resume their course, and fire
consume, whatever name you call it.

REVOLUTIONARY LETTER #51

As soon as we submit
to a system based on causality, linear time
we submit, again, to the old values, plunge again
into slavery. Be strong. We have the right to make
the universe we dream.
No need to fear "science"
                                    groveling
apology for things as they are, ALL POWER
TO JOY, which will remake the world.

REVOLUTIONARY LETTER #52

Don't give up the eleven o'clock news for
Chairman Mao, don't switch
from one "programming" to another
hang loose, Mao was young
fifty years ago, & in China.

REVOLUTIONARY LETTER #53

SAN FRANCISCO NOTE

I think I'll stay on this
earthquake fault near this
still-active volcano in this
armed fortress facing a
dying ocean &
covered w/ dirt
                    while the
streets burn up & the
rocks fly & pepper gas
lays us out
                    cause
that's where my friends are,
you bastards, not that
you know what that means

Ain't gonna cop to it, ain't gonna
be scared no more, we all
know the same songs, mushrooms, butterflies
                                        we all
have the same babies, dig it
the woods are big.

REVOLUTIONARY LETTER #54
HOW TO BECOME A WALKING ALCHEMICAL EXPERIMENT

eat *mercury* (in wheat & fish)
breathe *sulphur* fumes (everywhere)
take plenty of (macrobiotic) *salt*
& cook the mixture in the heat
of an atomic explosion

REVOLUTIONARY LETTER #55
IT TAKES COURAGE TO SAY NO

No to canned corn & instant
mashed potatoes. No to rice krispies.
No to Special K. No to margarine
mono- & di-glycerides, NSDA
for coloring, causing cancer. No to
white bread, bleached w/ nerve gas (wonder
bread). No to everything fried
in hardened oil w/ silicates. No to
once-so-delicious salami, now red
w/ sodium nitrate.

No to processed cheeses. No
no again to irradiated bacon, pink
phosphorescent ham, dead plastic
pasteurized milk. No to chocolate pudding
like grandma never made. No thanx
to coca-cola. No to freshness preservers,
dough conditioners, no
potassium sorbate, no
aluminum silicate, NO
BHA, BHT, NO
di-ethyl-propyl-glycerate.

No more ice cream? not w/ embalming fluid.
Goodbye potato chips, peanut butter, jelly, jolly
white sugar! No more DES
all-American steaks or hamburgers either!
Goodbye, frozen fish! (dipped & coated w/
aureomycin)   Fried eggs over easy w/
hormones, penicillin & speed.
Carnation Instant Breakfast, Nestle's Quik.
Fritos, goodbye! your labels are very confusing.

All I can say
is what my daughter age six once said to me:
*"if I can't pronounce it
maybe I shouldn't eat it."*

> or, Dick Gregory
> coming out of a 20-day fast:
>   *"the people of America are controlled
>   by the food they eat"*

REVOLUTIONARY LETTER #56

All thru Amerika
all I see & find is
Indian America
the forms & shapes of
Great-Turtle-Island

REVOLUTIONARY LETTER #57

The forms proliferate.
As we spin (further) from the light
our bodies sprout new madnesses
congenital pale disease, like new plants
on the edge of (radioactive) craters
we sprout new richness of design
baroque apologies for Kaliyuga
till Kether calls us home
hauls in the galaxies like some
big fish.

REVOLUTIONARY LETTER #58
NOTES TOWARD AN AMERICAN HISTORY

Over & over we look for
the picture in the cloth: man
standing idle & tall against
horizon: "savage" landscape
we stare, poverty-struck
at New England pewter in
farmhouse window: quote
Adams, Jefferson, hew
map of the sacred meadow

this *was* the
land we were promised,
wasnt it? is Fresno
new Jerusalem? where
is Dallas? how wd Olson/
Pound/ Tom Paine explain
Petaluma. Over & over Kirby Doyle
                                   mad
tells tale of his grandfather walking out
                                of the desert
his wife & two sons waiting in a wagon
                         (he had the mule)
                            & the boats
in Gloucester, Newfoundland & Greece
                            (the same)

the wood
carved in Alaska & New Guinea
                              (the same)

Over & over we seek that savage man
sufficient & generous;   we find
Rockefeller, Nixon;
                    sad letters of Jefferson
mourning the ravaging of moundbuilders' land
requesting his daughter not to neglect her French.
We; over & over; seeking line & form
gold-leaf as in Siena
"outline" as Blake
we sit on shifting ground
at the edge of this ocean
"as far from Europe as you can get"
& watch the hills flicker like dreamskin

REVOLUTIONARY LETTER #59

What we need to know is laws of time & space
they never dream of. Seek out
the ancient texts: alchemy
homeopathy, secret charts
of early Rosicrucians (Giordanisti).
Grok synchronicity Jung barely
            scratched the surface of.
LOOK TO THE "HERESIES" OF EUROPE FOR BLOODROOTS
    (remnants of pre-colonized pre-Roman Europe)
Insistent, hopeful resurgence of *communards*
free love & joy; "in god all things are common"
secret celebration of ancient season feasts & moons.
Rewrite the calendar.

Head-on war is the mistake we make
            time after time
There *is* a way around it, way to outflank
technology, short circuit
"energy crisis": retreat & silence
cunning
courage & love

REVOLUTIONARY LETTER #60

look to the cities, see how "urban renewal"
tears out the slums from the heart of town
forces expendable poor to the edges, to some
remote & indefensible piece of ground:
Hunters Point, Lower East Side, Columbia Point
out of sight, out of mind, & when bread riots come
(conjured by cutting welfare, raising prices)
the man wont hesitate to raze those ghettos
& few will see, & fewer will object.

REVOLUTIONARY LETTER #61

FIRST OBSERVABLE EFFECTS OF SO-CALLED "ENERGY CRISIS"
(FALL 1973)

1. offshore drilling renewed, Santa Barbara & elsewhere
   we can expect
   new wells to be opened
   regardless of consequences
2. price of crude oil shoots sky-high. making
   the extraction of shale oil feasible (profitable)
   which shale oil territory has been prepared
   for exploitation by forcing beef prices up, advocating
   beef boycotts, forcing
   smaller ranches toward bankruptcy
3. Peabody Coal plans to occupy Cheyenne land
   on legal grounds "natives" are "incapable"
   of exploiting its "natural resource," i.e.
   don't want to extract minerals at the cost
   of the land
4. grim austerity consciousness
   empty shelves & stiff upper lip
   & plenty of hoarding, reminiscent
   of early '40s, conditioned reflex
   right psychological climate for WW III
5. of course, police & military will have enough gas
   & how will *you* like
   to be stationary populace in the grip
   of a mobile army?

REVOLUTIONARY LETTER #62

Take a good look
at history (the American myth)
check sell out
of revolution by the founding fathers
"Constitution written by a bunch of gangsters
to exploit a continent" is what
                    Charles Olson told me.
Check Shay's rebellion, Aaron Burr, Nathan Hale.
Who wrote the history books where *you*
                    went to school?
Check Civil War: maybe industrial north
needed cheap labor, South had it, how many
sincere "movement" people
                    writers & radicals played
                    into their hands?
Check Haymarket trial: it broke the back
of strong Wobblie movement: how many jailed, fined
killed to stop that one? What's happening to us
has happened a few times before
                    let's change the script

What did it take to stop the Freedom Riders
What have we actually changed?
                    month I was born
they were killing onion pickers in Ohio

Month that I write this, nearly 40 years later
they're killing UFWs in the state
I'm trying somehow to live in. LET'S REWRITE
the history books
History repeats itself
only if we let it

REVOLUTIONARY LETTER #63

check Science: whose interest does it serve?
whose need to perpetrate
mechanical dead (exploitable) universe
instead of living cosmos?

whose dream those hierarchies: planets & stars
blindly obeying fixed laws, as they desire
us, too, to stay in place
whose interest to postulate
man's recent blind "descent" from "unthinking" animals
our pitiable geocentric isolation:
                              lone voice in the stars

what point in this cosmology but to drain
hope of contact or change
                              oppressing us w/ "reason"

REVOLUTIONARY LETTER #64
for Camilla Hall

The holocaust
    moves
towards its own
        ends.

The rose will bloom
  in the lotus pond.

The lotus will flower
  on the rose tree.

In the enclosed garden
    which is
the garden of mirrors
a temple of mist
    rises.

REVOLUTIONARY LETTER #65
for Tim Leary

> *Let everything private be made public.* —Charles Olson

Let everything private be made public!
We have had enough of secrecy, paid assassins, radio
      controlled robots, mysterious disappearances, planted
      evidence, men's doubles arrested in their stead in
      funky rooming houses whose landladies disappear
thinly-veiled race war, fake shortages, inflation, night raids,
      manipulated famine,
transistors in brain, overdoses of tranqs, truth scrum,
      interrogation.
It is very boring to spend the 1970s in Nazi Germany, or
      Stalinist Russia
we have already seen this movie & it don't look better / in color.
Even they must be tired of it, these latter-day Nazis, skulking
      & posing, plotting & counterplotting, each suspicious
      of the other
PROGRAM TO RELIEVE THEIR MURKY BRAIN-CELLS
      & THE SOULS OF ALL SENTIENT BEINGS:
Out w/ it, brothers! Let's everybody tell everything they know
We'll have a press conference in the form of ancient confession
      where each can absolve his fellow. It may take a decade
      but in the end: no prisons, no schools, no madhouses,
      no IRS, no IBM, no ITT, no government!
A decade well-spent . . . .

REVOLUTIONARY LETTER #66
TO THE PATRIARCHS
  for Inez García

> *"That a man's body is
> in itself a weapon in a
> way that a woman's body
> is not."* —Free Inez García Committee

My body a weapon as yours is
MY CHILDREN WEAPONS ETERNALLY
My tits weapons against the immaterial

My strong thighs
    choking the black lie
My hips
    haven & fort
    place where I stand
    & from which I fight

My war is concentrated in the noise
    of my hair
My hands
    lethal to imprecision
My cunt a bomb exploding
    yr christian conscience

My teeth tear out the throat of yr despair
My jaws annihilate computer centuries
My arms/my knees embrace yr serpent
    yr sin becomes my song

The shock waves of my pleasure
    annihilate
all future shock
all future shock forever

REVOLUTIONARY LETTER #67

ANOTHER WYOMING SONG

silk sari is famine.
prayer is famine.
stone idol washed by seawind
                also famine
song on crumbling streets
                is famine
moonstone necklace
sandalwood essence
perfect buddha caves—all famine
teddy bear in Macy's window, famine
tobacco bursting from Virginia soil
coal mines famine, oil field famine
new car famine
I got the toe-nail, boot-sole, bootlegging wagon famine
    cracked lips & all.
yesterday famine
tomorrow famine
iron wind breaking up the sandy ground like famine
    like hunger to the heart.
got let's-turn-these-stones-to-bread famine
burnt baby famine
                wish I knew
                & you do too
how to avert, turn aside
African famine
Egyptian famine
Sioux famine

Navaho famine
Mesopotamian famine
Easter Island famine
Tahitian famine
Sumerian famine
Sonoran famine
Hindu famine
mountain famine
woodland famine
desert famine
tundra famine
great plains famine
Papago famine
Evanston famine
Chicago famine
Casper famine
Bozeman-to-Billings famine
Minneapolis famine
Nevada sagebrush famine
Little Italy famine
Harlem famine
Chinatown famine
Tibetan famine
Third World famine
fourth dimension famine
fifth estate famine
hungry ghost famine
black panther famine
Oakland famine
Omaha famine

Amazon famine
Machu Picchu famine
alcohol famine
opium famine
Bengali famine
Brooklyn famine
ALL THE BELLIES IS SWOLLEN
   some from too much
   some from too little
all like to burst—only the crows, no famine
hyenas not hungry
buzzards not hungry
jackal, coyote, eagle
             filling up
a feast before they die
   like we die
on dying land

REVOLUTIONARY LETTER #68
LIFE CHANT

> *may it come that all the radiances*
> *will be known as our own radiance*
> *—Tibetan Book of the Dead*

cacophony of small birds at dawn
        may it continue
sticky monkey flowers on bare brown hills
        may it continue
bitter taste of early miner's lettuce
        may it continue
music on city streets in the summer nights
        may it continue
kids laughing on roofs on stoops on the beach in the snow
        may it continue
triumphal shout of the newborn
        may it continue
deep silence of great rainforests
        may it continue
fine austerity of jungle peoples
        may it continue
rolling fuck of great whales in turquoise ocean
        may it continue
clumsy splash of pelican in smooth bays
        may it continue
astonished human eyeball squinting thru aeons at astonished
                    nebulae who squint back
        may it continue

clean snow on the mountain
>   may it continue

fierce eyes, clear light of the agèd
>   may it continue

rite of birth & of naming
>   may it continue

rite of instruction
>   may it continue

rite of passage
>   may it continue

love in the morning, love in the noon sun
love in the evening among crickets
>   may it continue

long tales by fire, by window, in fog, in dusk on the mesa
>   may it continue

love in thick midnight, fierce joy of old ones loving
>   may it continue

the night music
>   may it continue

grunt of mating hippo, giraffe, foreplay of snow leopard
>   screeching of cats on the backyard fence
>   may it continue

without police
>   may it continue

without prisons
>   may it continue

without hospitals, death medicine: flu & flu vaccine
>   may it continue

without madhouses, marriage, highschools that are prisons
>   may it continue

without empire
                    may it continue
in sisterhood
                    may it continue
thru the wars to come
                    may it continue
in brotherhood
                    may it continue
tho the earth seem lost
                    may it continue
thru exile & silence
                    may it continue
with cunning & love
                    may it continue
as woman continues
                    may it continue
as breath continues
                    may it continue
as stars continue
                    may it continue

may the wind deal kindly w/ us
may the fire remember our names
may springs flow, rain fall again
may the land grow green, may it swallow our mistakes

we begin the work
                    may it continue
the great transmutation
                    may it continue
a new heaven & a new earth
                    may it continue
                    may it continue

REVOLUTIONARY LETTER #69
MATAGALPA, 1978

These eyes of children   closer
than fingernail set
                              in my hand
these
         maimed villages closer
than my heart
                         beating
                                        pressing
against my lungs

                         A form of love
all touch is
                  and what
does not touch something?
                                        at least
the air   the ground

                         These eyes
of triumphant children
                                   the blood
bursts thru
                  as the gentle
                                   villages
are strafed
                  the blood
                              bone   muscle

burning
      but the forests
            are full
the deserts
      on the move
            the jungles
whisper RESIST.
         The eyeballs
of children burst
      w/ blood
          & love
& the cities
      of America
         the center
of the killer tornado
        the cities   yes
the cities of
      Amerika fill
         w/ Resistance
the dream
      of old men & women
           stranded
on her sidewalks
      seeking food, seeking
          freedom
finding
    only insult
         EVEN THESE CITIES ARE FULL
of triumphant resistance

                      & the dream of the old
is echoed in the young.

                   "All artists
are warriors"
             sd my son & he
age eight
        is sure.

Eyes of the children
               Managua
               New York
               Matagalpa
               Houston
               Soweto
               Manila
               Tehran
               Bogota
               Oakland
                         eyes & hands
Knives & guns
            of the children
                     Peru
                     Zimbabwe
                     Mexico
eyes & hands
            knives & guns
                   of the children

These eyes of children
                        windows
                                    on our hope:
that
    ALL RESISTANCE IS
                            TRIUMPHANT RESISTANCE.
All love
       is revolution
& all touch
       a form of love

The moment of revolt is the moment of victory.

REVOLUTIONARY LETTER #70

FROM SAN FRANCISCO
   for Harvey Milk and George Moscone

out of the heaps of the bodies of "suicides," as we must call
all suicides who have leaped to incarnation on this planet
                              out of the stench of jungle-exploded
flesh, pall and haze of what we conceive as destruction;
                                             in the stunned and muted clamor
of a city which has lost for whatever reason its mayor, and
(unprecedented) a loved politician
                                          as the solstice struggles, as
every year, toward darkness, and the nights are longer than
sleep and only the bright clangor of Orion's wardrobe rings
in the dusty sky
                        in the resurgence of fifties paranoia—thirties
paranoia—sixties paranoia—which generation do you claim?—
it comes clear
                this dark is the light we love by, and that we love at
all a miracle in the cloned styrofoam wastes & desolations
of our lives.
                    This dark a song of burgeoning difference, flesh at
least, and loved and loving however blindly—See the dance:
                                          we may disdain
Castro Street, curse the baths, criticize the women's movement,
turn our backs on revolution, mock the growth awareness
human potential bullshit, but it is song and passion when
set against the worlds of middle America middle Russia
Hinduism Islam China.

We spin out light in a dark time, grow it
at cost out of the incandescence of flesh we still call living, and
all the fingers of the night point home to us.

Think: the cauldron
of rebirth in which the robot dead return to life, from which
they burst at dawn to the same hollow battle—this is the tale
spun out and spun again, the *only* tale the media tells your
children

that we reach out hand to hand or twine our ankles
in our chilly beds is breath of shame to a nation gone to death:
rigor mortis the grin of their pride, the stiff necks of 900 corpses
a metaphor they drink

hungry as Aztecs to still the movement
in the skies. Whose hand moves in Iran, who is choking the
Eskimo in his condominium, sets the Angolan in his compound
drives the Maasai sterile? But that is old news, and only the
pygmy flutes carry it to the stars.

That, and an occasional
eagle bone whistle of the Ute straggling thru the last sundance
in the high plains.

On whose world is the sun going down
sisters and brothers? Dare we claim it, dare we lose it again?
But that is old news, and it is whispered that *sol invictus* is only
invictus so far.

It is no longer relevant—who cares if the CIA was
disposing of plutonium thru People's Temple, or Emmet
Grogan was offed on a subway train? The plots and subplots
rauwolfia and DMSO, carcinoma 256, the discreetly revealed
and scattered dreams of the nouveau-Borgia

                    petty Napoleons
who've forgotten Egypt, emasculated robber barons sucking
their wives' lovers' cocks in the boiler room

                             in the dark all
news is old news, the only glimmer the lambent marshlight of
our flesh as we gesture towards difference, a burgeoning race
of mutants

               gorging on drugs, come, California wine, richness
of fruit and meat on a planet spinning toward famine

                              perverse
and mushrooming cadence of phosphorescent loves, falling
to compost as the sun goes out.

                      We greet the dark.

REVOLUTIONARY LETTER #71

FOR BELLA AKHMADULINA

> *In her great poem "I Swear",
> written for her forerunner, the poet
> Marina Tsvetaeva, Bella Akhmadulina
> vows to "kill Yelabuga", the town in
> which Tsvetaeva hanged herself in
> 1941. Akhmadulina addresses the town
> as if it were some kind of malevolent
> entity or demon.*

A life for a life, a young black
woman's voice said to me on the
phone the day George
Jackson died in prison and I
said even twenty, a hundred for that
one would be cheap. Even a thousand.
And if I claimed a million
lives for each of my lost, like some
superHitler out to depopulate
the earth, and cd drink, somehow
that blood: this one's
for you, Freddie, and this for you,
Lee Probst, Genevieve, Gloria still
alive but dead and you, Little One
we called you & this immensity
of gore I drink to you, Jimmy, teacher
and friend. O lost mad Mike, killed brain of Timothy, palsy
in Allen's face, this one's
for Warren Miller, nobody knows

they killed. Fred Hampton in his bed, asleep
in blood. Emmett who told us
it wdn't be "overdose" that got him,
a million lives for each
so what, it wd take four thousand only
to finish us all then & I alone
cd probably name four thousand.
Listen.
There's got to be another way, we can't
just kill *Yelabuga* or be killed. Or both.
There's
anyway here, the ghost dance, or tin
floating as gold in the vessel. I know it's nonsense
but is it worse nonsense than drinking yourself to death
tonight in some Russian suburb? Here
we've got Black Elk's four horses in the sky
to replace the ones in Revelations. What
have you got? You must have *something*
I won't be "translated"
alone, or at least w/ out female
buddies, I know some of the men will "buy" the ideal
but they don't count, they never carried their flesh
grave as lead, there must be a peasant whisper
the shape of a hill, or a sneaky look
in the eyes of an ancient icon—give me a hint
don't hide
& die
          there isn't enough blood on earth
to buy our losses. And blood is salt, it will never
quench my thirst. Do we kill,

or split
      or kill & split
             or translate this shit
to a paradise omitting nothing taking nothing
w/ us.   Gravid, full
of the squirming seeds of our dead

can we
sow the wind?
can we
condense fury till it is
flame
      can we use this fuel
to move us out of here

                  a flying leap
to another "plane" or "sphere"
& I don't *know* into what, don't ask, only
I know it won't be *worse*

REVOLUTIONARY LETTER #72
A SPELL FOR THE CHILDREN OF THE POOR

Here
is a camera for Obsidian
of Thunder Mountain, Nevada, tour guide
who cares for her mother & all
her brothers & sisters, whose eyes
turn always toward the highway   & a

lifetime supply of charcoal & pens
& brushes for Melissa, black girl who lives
next door to me in the Fillmore where the grocer
refuses to give her eggs if she's 2¢ short   & she's
always
2¢ short,   her mom
spent the last five dollars on codeine
'cause she hurts   &

notebooks by the dozen for Erlinda
Shakespeare,   Shoshone,   age 12 who was
afraid to write more on her great
long poem 'cause the notebook we gave her
(Poetry In The Schools,   1972) was running out &
notebooks
          cost 35¢

There *is* enough paper
Erlinda, and paint, and a violin
for your brother
                          & all the leotards
anybody wants
                     on Webster St, in
Hunters Point.
                   Here's a drum set
another   take the whole damn
music store
                what are we
holding onto when you guys

are the only art that's News

REVOLUTIONARY LETTER #73
DREAM POEM ABOUT REAGAN & CO

when we are dirt poor
and no longer have our mountains for shelter
when we are conquered
and cannot go to our forests for comfort
when we are hungry
and our valleys will no longer sustain us
then we will see these men
in their true light

REVOLUTIONARY LETTER #74
for Fulcanelli & John Lennon

There is always   the fire.   Downwind it
blows our eyebrows off, blows holes
in our dusty skin.   In the crucible
it melts our faces into knots & puddles
It melts our hearts.   And they become rock or
something more *feeling* than flesh.   There is
no way around it, it *is*   there is
always
            the fire.   Is this alchemy?   Must
the process pass thru
                              10,000 suns? There
has never been a way
around
            the crucible.   Can the heat
of our love excel
                        tangible flame? Only then
can *this* crucible
                  replace
                              the old.   There are
even in alchemy "two ways" and this
our way *can* supplant
habits of war.   It is
                              "the dry way"
                                          (no blood,
no tears)   only
                        substantial presence,
my hand in yours.
                        And you a stranger.

There are no
strangers.   Now.
                            This transformation
by the Inward Fire
                    (our heat / our love)
                                        no
charred limbs, blistered eyeballs, brain
turned to steam
                only
                    the Inward Fire,   slow
combustion / quick change / tomorrow
is already here.

REVOLUTIONARY LETTER #75
RANT

You cannot write a single line w/ out a cosmology
a cosmogony
laid out, before all eyes

there is no part of yourself you can separate out
saying, this is memory, this is sensation
this is the work I care about, this is how I
make a living

it is whole, it is a whole, it always was whole
you do not "make" it so
there is nothing to integrate, you are a presence
you are an appendage of the work, the work stems from
hangs from the heaven you create

every man / every woman carries a firmament inside
& the stars in it are not the stars in the sky

w/ out imagination there is no memory
w/ out imagination there is no sensation
w/ out imagination there is no will, desire

history is a living weapon in yr hand
& you have imagined it, it is thus that you
"find out for yourself"
history is the dream of what can be, it is
the relation between things in a continuum

of imagination
what you find out for yourself is what you select
out of an infinite sea of possibility
no one can inhabit yr world

yet it is not lonely,
the ground of imagination is fearlessness
discourse is video tape of a movie of a shadow play
but the puppets are in yr hand
your counters in a multidimensional chess
which is divination
                        & strategy

the war that matters is the war against the imagination
all other wars are subsumed in it.

the ultimate famine is the starvation
of the imagination

it is death to be sure, but the undead
seek to inhabit someone else's world

the ultimate claustrophobia is the syllogism
the ultimate claustrophobia is "it all adds up"
nothing adds up & nothing stands in for
anything else

THE ONLY WAR THAT MATTERS IS THE WAR AGAINST THE
IMAGINATION
THE ONLY WAR THAT MATTERS IS THE WAR AGAINST THE
IMAGINATION
THE ONLY WAR THAT MATTERS IS THE WAR AGAINST THE
IMAGINATION
ALL OTHER WARS ARE SUBSUMED IN IT

There is no way out of the spiritual battle
There is no way you can avoid taking sides
There is no way you can *not* have a poetics
no matter what you do: plumber, baker, teacher

you do it in the consciousness of making
or not making yr world
you have a poetics: you step into the world
like a suit of readymade clothes

or you etch in light
your firmament spills into the shape of your room
the shape of the poem, of yr body, of yr loves

A woman's life / a man's life is an allegory

Dig it

There is no way out of the spiritual battle
the war is the war against the imagination
you can't sign up as a conscientious objector

the war of the worlds hangs here, right now, in the balance
it is a war for this world, to keep it
a vale of soul-making

the taste in all our mouths is the taste of our power
and it is bitter as death

bring yr self home to yrself, enter the garden
the guy at the gate w/ the flaming sword is yrself

the war is the war for the human imagination
and no one can fight it but you / & no one can fight it for you

The imagination is not only holy, it is precise
it is not only fierce, it is practical
men die every day for the lack of it,
it is vast & elegant

intellectus   means "light of the mind"
it is not discourse it is not even language
the inner sun

the *polis* is constellated around the sun
the fire is central

REVOLUTIONARY LETTER #76

GESTAPO POEM

Where is gestapo, where
does it end? Where
is it? Soweto, it is. Where
does it end? Not
Oakland, it doesn't
not B'nai Brith.

Where
is it? Gaza, it is. Where
is it? San Quentin, it is. Where?
Peru. Where? Paris. Where? in Bonn
& Prague & Beijing, it is
in Yellow River Valley. Where
is it? Afghan, Guatemala, Rio,
Alaska, Tierra del Fuego, the
wasted *taiga*, it is
where is it?
& where
does it end.
          Not in
Oakland, it doesn't,
not in London. Not in the Mission.
Don't end in Brooklyn
or Rome. Atlanta. Where?
Morocco, gestapo is
Sudan (& death)
Where end? not Canada sold to

Nazi USA
not Mexico, Kenya, Australia
it don't, not end
Jamaica, Haiti. Mozambique
not end. Maybe
someplace it isn't maybe
someplace it ends
some hills maybe
still free
          but hungry
                    (eyes

blaze
     over ancient guns

REVOLUTIONARY LETTER #77
AWKWARD SONG ON THE EVE OF WAR

The center of my heart is Arab song.
It is woven around my heartstrings
I cannot uproot it.
It is the song of the Beloved as Other
The Other as God, it is all about Light
and we never stop singing it.

The root of my brain
(the actual stem and medulla)
is the Tree of Life.
It is the story we have all been telling
The story of the journey and return
It is all about Light
and we never stop telling it.

I cannot uproot this Tree from the back of my head
I cannot tear this Song out of my heart
I cannot allow the two to war in my cells.

This is a prose poem and it is didactic

It remembers the perfumes of Lebanon, lapis of Persia
The mountains, ziggurats, ladders of ascent
The hut in the field we entered as Her body.

The fabric of our seeing is dark & light
Ahriman / Ahura   the two lobes

of the brain. Or yin and yang.
The paintings of Turkestan echo in caves
of North China. The Manichee's eyes are carved
in Bone Oracles.

I cannot cut the light from my eyes
or the woven shadow from the curves of my brain.

The dance of the *I Ching* is the dance of the star tide
Mathematics of the Zend Avesta
Geometries of Ife
There is only one Sun and it is just rising

The golden ikon of the Black Virgin
stands at the stone gateway of Tashkent.
The flowering valleys of Shambhala
haunt our dreaming.
What skeletons stalk there?

Do you see?

If even the plants send out warnings to each other
If even the brine shrimp mourn each other's passing . . .

My eyes stare from ten thousand Arab faces
A deer sniffs at the stiffening corpse of her yearling.

There is only one Sun and it is rising
It is much too strong in the desert of our minds.

Shield us from the desert of greed
The desert of hate
Shield us from the desert of chauvinism
Le désert désespèré
Desperate desert of no song, no image
Shield us from the desert of no return

That Arab song burst out of mountain cave
That fine-worked silver glisten in the sun

> *Loving, yes, loving, woman, and*
> *digging on each other*
> *thousands of years,*
> *digging the differences. . . .*

Let the gold-clad men and women
dark skins gleaming
dance at the stone gates:
      Shiprock, New Grange, Tashkent
Let the goddess walk again on the African plains
      The Orisha brighten the air

There is only one Sun and it is rising.
May the peaches of Samarkand bloom in the Okanagan.

Reprise:
There is nothing we have been that we will be
None of the myths suffices.

Let us read each other's maps at the foot of the Tree
Where the stream of Song moves out in all directions.

REVOLUTIONARY LETTER #78
BULLETIN

It is happening even as you read this page. By the time you finish reading this it will be over.

She will have left the hotel and disappeared. He will have eaten the pills. That one will slip and crack her skull on the floor. That one will go out in a driveby shooting.

halfway around the world the bombs are dropping

As you read these words it is already too late. 200,000 children will have starved. One of them held the Jewel in his brain, another could cure plagues with her breath.

As you read this line one thousand have died of AIDS. They die alone hidden in furnished rooms. They die on the earth all over Africa.

halfway around the world the bombs are falling

Do not think to correct this by refusing to read.
It happens as you put down the paper, head for the door.
The ozone reaches the point of no-return

the butterflies bellyflop, the last firefly, etc.
Do not think to correct this by reading.

The bombs burst the small skull of an Arab infant the silky black hair is stuck to your hands with brains. W/ bits of blood. There is less shrieking than you would expect

A soft silence. The silence of the poor, those who could not afford to leave. Drop flowers on them from yr mind, why don't you? "I guess we'll have to stay and take our chances."

They die so silently even as we speak

Black eyes of children seek eyes of the dying mother
bricks fall dirt spurts like fountains in the streets.
In the time you fill a cup they die of thirst.

In the time it takes to turn off the radio.
Not past, not future

The huts are blazing *now*. South of Market a woman ODs with an elegant sigh. No more no less than is needed.

halfway around the world the bombs are dropping

REVOLUTIONARY LETTER #79
ONE OF THE JOBS OF CRONEDOM
(on the eve of the first Gulf War)

Some of us have to mourn
while the rest of you
organize.

Some of us have to dance
in the time of grief.

REVOLUTIONARY LETTER #80
GOOD CLEAN FUN

It's terrorism, isn't it, when you're afraid to answer the door for
                                        lack of a Green Card
afraid to look for work, walk into the hospital when yr child
                                        is sick,

and what else than terrorism cd you call those smallpox
                                        blankets we gave the Indians
the trail of tears, the raids on Ghost Dancing tribes
It's terrorism when you're forbidden to speak yr language
paddled for it, made to run a hundred laps in the snow
in your thin & holey sneakers. What do you call it
when you're locked in yr high school classroom, armed
                                        policemen
manning the halls? Isn't it terrorism to force a young woman
to talk to her parents abt her clandestine love
the child she will or will not carry? Is it terrorism
to shoot striking onion workers (1934), pick off AIM members
                                        one by one?

What happened to the Hampton family in Chicago—
                    Fred Hampton blown away in his bed—
would you call that terrorism? Or the MOVE kids in
                                        Philadelphia
bombed in their home. Or all the stories we *don't* know
buried in throats stuffed w/ socks, or pierced w/ bullets.
Wd you call it terrorism, what happened at Wounded Knee
or the Drug Wars picking off

the youth of our cities—as they already picked off
twenty years ago—or terrified into silence—the ones who shd
                              be leading us now—
you know the names.

What was COINTELPRO if not terrorism? What new initials
                    are they calling it today?

Is Leonard Peltier a victim of terrorism?
Is Mumia Abu-Jamal?

Is it terrorism if you are terrified
of the INS, the IRS, the landlord, yr boss, the man
who might do yr job for less?
if you're scared of yr health insurance
no health insurance
scared of yr street, yr hallway, scared every month
you might not get to the 1st and the next measly check?

Is it terrorism to take food from hungry school-kids?
To threaten teenagers who still have hope enough
have joy enough to bring babies into this mess?

How has terrorism touched *you*, shaped *your* life?
Are you afraid to go out, to walk in yr city, yr suburb, yr
                                        countryside?
To read, to speak yr own language, wear yr tribe's clothes?
Afraid of the thin-shelled birds w/ twisted necks
poisoned by nitrates, by selenium?
Afraid that the dawn will be silent, the forests grey?

Is it terrorism to fill the Dnieper River w/ radiation?
or heat the ionosphere w/ magnetism "to see what will
happen"?
>   *A wonderful weapon, they say, it will perturb*
>   *the weather pattern, disrupt communications*
Who are the terrorists in the lumber wars?
(the water wars are coming)
And we haven't even talked about AIDS and cancer.

IS THE ASSAULT ON NATIVE INTELLIGENCE & GOOD WILL
THAT WE CALL THE EVENING NEWS
ANYTHING OTHER THAN AN ACT OF TERROR?

What was the Gulf War but terrorism
wearing the death mask of order?—one big car bomb it was
the guys who drove it dying now
one by one—ignored

Is acid rain a form of terrorism? (Think for yourself.)
Is GATT or NAFTA anything but a pact among brigands—
the World Bank, the IMF their back-up men?
How long before they fight over the spoils? Who'll do their
fighting for them?

Is Alan Greenspan perhaps the biggest *known & named*
of our terrorist leaders, *here*, nurtured *here*,
trained *here*

the dark design of whose hearts makes
Hutu & Tutsi
Croat & Muslim & Serb
mere diversionary tactics before the onslaught

REVOLUTIONARY LETTER #81
ON THE WAY HOME
(A Prayer for the Road)

On the way home
all the restaurants will serve miso soup

On the way home
exotic notebook stores will blossom in small towns in Nevada

On the way home
Utah will be festooned w/ mirth
Mormons will be dancing in the streets in gauzy *chatchkas*

On the way home
Everyone will leave the casinos and the slot machines & go
                                                    outside
to stare at the beauty of the mountains, of the sky, of each other

On the way home
All the boys & girls in the secret desert bordellos
will have set up temples of free love festooned with mimosa
they will teach karma-mudra to joyful redneck ranchers
who have set all their cows free and now drink only amrita

On the way home
every cafe in Wyoming will be holding a potlatch
poverty will thus be abolished

On the way home
everyone we meet will try to read us a poem
invite us in for a story there being no news
but what travellers bring, all TV having died

On the way home
it will be easy to find pure water, organic tomatoes, friendly
                                                    conversation
We'll give & receive delightful music & blessings at every
                                                    gas station

(all the gas will be free)

On the way home
all the truck drivers will drive politely
the traveling summer tourists will beam at their kids

our old Toyota will love going up mountain passes
openhearted & unsuspicious people & lizards
prairie dogs, wolves & magpies will sing together & picnic
at sunset beside the road

Everyone will get where they're going
Everyone will be peaceful
Everyone will like it when they get there

All obstacles smoothed
auspiciousness & pleasure
will sit like a raven dakini
on every roof

REVOLUTIONARY LETTER #82
Avenging
       angels

sticks of dynamite   wrapped
   in   baby
blankets
         baby
blue
        like their eyes
not
   human
elemental
       eyes
spewing
     fire
carbines
      shot
guns
   it doesn't   matter
pale
   pixie
       faces
elfin
   smiles
laughing
       I've always
wanted
      to   do
           this

wanted
      to see you
dead   o   comrade
see   me   dead
o   beautiful
          long-legged   maiden
o   sour-faced
          teacher of   woodshop
of home
          economics

always
          wanted
to   see   you
          dead as a
door   nail
          as this bomb
full of nails
          blasting
so beautiful
          into   the wood
the glass
          the   plaster
into
          flesh

red
   as tampons
or   lipstick

           o beautiful
black-eyed
           maiden
dark
      skin.   like
madrone
      blood   like
rivers
river   canyons
which echo
      only echo
      only   repeat
nothing
      is added
the ground
      is   dead
the air
      you   see?
dead   also
                 these shots

awaken
      ghosts
or spirits
      in the arms
of bare
      trees marked
for death
      the scream
of the saws

scream of
the logging trucks
subway
scream
out of all yr
throats
ivory
brown
or golden
young or old
air dead
the rivers
marked for death
this
scream
spatter
of bullets brings
air
alive
for a moment
something
alive

I stand w/ my friends
this gallant
force

           young / dead
long / lost
               condemned
to a pittance
               of hope
we stand proud
               give back
the legacy

dead ground
          dead
mother
          dead
rivers
     & empty
plains

     O the full lips
hard thighs
     beloved
comrades
     whose black
daring
     cuts a path
for
     rivers
of blood
     buys red
life for a
     moment   w/

death
    yours
mine
my
it   doesn't
      matter not
really
   I avenge
the babies
   beaten
the mother
   w/ dead sex
dead eyes
   I avenge
myself
   violated
spitted
   on ancient
rotted   cocks
avenge
   the   planet
torn
   & bloody

This charnel ground
    we were born
into
   dancing
ground
   O beautiful

lads & lasses
    we mourn

              we buy
life
   fountains
         of   fire
light
   Roman candles of
                blood

                  bits   of
flesh
   moving
IN MOTION
for once
   this trajectory
is vast
   not   simple
pain
   dead   grey
prairie
   grey
skies
   become
          instead
a shower of
        sparks
fountain

                  O beautiful
         fountains
             & rivers
       of   blood.

REVOLUTIONARY LETTER #83

IN THE WINK OF AN EYE:
Millennial Notes

    If Iliad & Odyssey encompass two sides of the great
divide—great break w/ the mythic & rise of the wily

    Then *polymetis* Odysseus—still a sacred king tho living
in the west (*zophos*) & with shards (shades) of the old time
clinging to his robes

    degenerates into *pius Aeneas*—the careful old fart,
practical family man & we are lost to ourselves for 1,000
or more years

    till the aching DULLNESS is too much to bear & we
emerge into Tantra

    the way of *ecstasis*: Rumi to Vidal & the Dull Party gets
freaked & burns up Provence

    and old Dante arises to put a cap on the fire, impose
some order on ecstasy

  and Willie the Shake tries to see: cd they co-exist? ecstasy
& order—harmony & godseeking freak-out

    & he doesn't solve it but he makes some kind of
Trembling Equation—

    And Blake sez, fuck all this, fuck coexistence, we need,
we do need a new spiritual order—& proceeds to make
one, sweeping the Romantics along in his wake

    And Baudelaire agrees, but won't come out to play, tries
to make a new order inside the shell of the old

But Rimbaud *sees* w/ his seer's eyes that we are already in it, the spirit, & stark raving naked—we'll have to leave everything behind

& at first he is thrilled but then cops out—it's too chilly in outer space w/ no clothes he'd rather die a sleaze-butt but *human* for God's sake

There is only one place to go from there, Thelema—The new spiritual order for real, a western *terma*, complete with crazy wisdom, the Holy Books

And sometimes, just sometimes the American cats move in on it they don't know from order they don't know from clothes—naked in space is OK w/ Melville,

Whitman don't know from leave behind, blasted with vastness & forlorn w/ blood sickness

this is more than existential crisis
"just SPACE"
& Pound & Olson bring history along for the ride, the ocean currents & how we followed them

so that Troy falls again, or doesn't this time—doesn't this whole thing happen cause Troy fell

men stopped wearing perfume & silk
brightness fell from the air
the Lady of Heaven got bored, went underground
it is

a crisis of spirit—&

the leap out of it   beyond it
our most recent shot
"just SPACE" = Thelema

                    Hermetic
Definition

a different color
different light in the mind

REVOLUTIONARY LETTER #84
FEBRUARY 14, 2001

someone
put out a flag
for Valentine's Day, as if
the domain of the heart
could belong
to this heartbroken nation—

REVOLUTIONARY LETTER #85
MOUNT HEBRON

Shall we
gentlemen
go home now
for the night   the

very long night?
The Shekinah sent word
she won't be coming

REVOLUTIONARY LETTER #86
SHORT POEMS ON THE AFGHAN WAR

1.
small bones of
mountain children
in the snow

2.
bags of rice burst open
burlap flaps in the wind
even the label "USA" is fading

3.
<u>We Airdrop Transistor Radios</u>

can you eat them?
will they
keep you warm?

REVOLUTIONARY LETTER #87
LES AMÉRICAINS

we are feral   rare
as mountain wolves
our hearts are pure
& stupid   we go down

pitted against our own

REVOLUTIONARY LETTER #88
NOTES TOWARD A POEM OF REVOLUTION

> *It is better to lose and win*
> *than win and be defeated.*
> —Gertrude Stein

1.
What did we in all honesty expect?
That fascist architecture flaunting
    @ the sky
converted now to fluid
       toxic
smoke, ASH
the long finger of
          impermanence
touches us all   & nobody
can hog the marbles & expect
the others to play

2.
While we mourn & rant for years
over our 3000   how many
                starve
thanks to our greed
          our unappeasable
hunger

3.
WATER is rising
WIND is blowing

gonna strip the last of
                              our
cheap & awkward
cities

only the music
some of the music
remains

4.
voice of my daughter
quivering on the phone
as she watches
the towers burn

from her new apartment
the one w/ the view . . .

5.
Gulf War, '91, my son
                @ the demonstration
stops by
            to eat

Well, we took out
a recruiting station
he tells me
while the cops
followed the crowd downtown
a group of us
split off.

                I nod &
bite my tongue.   Why talk about
what happened the year he was born?

6.
Wanted a northwest passage
& you've got it, Magellan!
Henry Hudson, A-mer-eee-go,
Da Gama,   are you proud
                        all of you
it took us
only 500 years to melt
that Polar ice

7.
And is it suicide when penguins
Give up?   Lie down

8.
Children sold in Africa
in India
child labor laws held barely
eighty years   now
eight-year-olds in brothels   dead
eyes
          who invented
this hell?

9.
Black holes in our hearts
ground zero
          our minds   hands
that won't open   let
                    go

10.
Tell me again how many janitors
died in the Towers
                    how many
          sandwich makers'
toilet cleaners'
          families will get that
two-million-per-victim
          in aid?

11.
lost Montségur, we did
lost Prague   the German
peasant uprisings   lost
Andalusia   (twice)
the Paris Commune
lost at Haymarket
          lost
Paul Robeson   Spain
even lost   Dashiell Hammett
lost San Francisco   fairly
recently

12.
Chuck in his shorts
watering his garden

gunned down in the Mill Valley
dawn

13.
we hole up
enclaves who speak
(again)   in whispers

as they did
when I first came
to these cities

14.
don't mourn
don't organize

strike & move on

REVOLUTIONARY LETTER #89
INDEPENDENCE DAY 2002

bald eagle
making a come-back

so am I

REVOLUTIONARY LETTER #90
ANCIENT HISTORY

The women are lying down
in front of the bulldozers
sent to destroy
the last of the olive groves.

REVOLUTIONARY LETTER #91
for Gerrit Lansing

"I" vanish
as the witness
always vanishes.
After the fact.

The Buddha is
the "thus come"
but the mark
of the Magus
is   "to go"

same word.

REVOLUTIONARY LETTER #92

SECOND GULF WAR

WIND tears at the city like the nervous fingers of an invalid
unraveling an afghan like the choppy waves of a small New
Jersey lake leaving oil scum along the shore Wind picks
up plastic bags rolls syringes around in the gutter ruffles
feathers of hungry pigeons chomping on *Street Sheet* BRING
OUR WAR HOME it says & a skinny girl waves her small fist
at the heavens Now you *read* it, hear? said the guy when I
gave him my dollar We gotta he says bring the war home
like it says Oh I'll read it all right I tell him, it's not me
you gotta convince I continue under my breath Wind
turns a corner rips the camellias off a kind of hedge behind
which an american flag hangs discreetly azaleas come apart
ranunculus and iceland poppies hold their own Windows
rattle pipes bang a tea kettle screeches just so we know inside
is no safer than out a breeze moves circumspectly thru the
loft and the ficus prepares to drop its leaves

DON'T read the paper listen to the news the names I'm
trying to remember were never written not even in
cuneiform never written not spoke so's you cd pronounce
them consonants so different the ear cannot distinguish—
anguish or laughter is that?—flute tabor what kind of
drum no point in learning that alphabet now it's dust the
WIND rules particulate matter from pyres from burning oil
wells crushed clay tablets older than the names we know
it wd be a mistake to confuse these gods with Ceres with
Demeter even Isis

THEY go are gone with their own riding lions carrying
emblems we can't decipher *Charm smiling at good mouth*
that was Kirby Doyle cremated a mere 36 hours ago
Missing In Action more poets than you imagine more
street urchins teen hustlers with sores that haven't healed
since the Gulf War only the mothers are NOT missing
mostly they can't afford that luxury STAY why don't you
and rip your chador into bandages STAY and distill pure
water from sweat or tears *Quick eyes gone under earth's lid*
that wd be Brakhage now ten days gone stop we need look
no further the most brutal wars are fought on this our own
dead soil the WIND carries as dust to our nostrils / hearts

for two gross of broken statues
a few thousand battered books

REVOLUTIONARY LETTER #93

MEMORIAL DAY, 2003

> *Today is Memorial Day. Take time to remember*
> *those brave souls who gave their lives for freedom.*
> —Dear Abby, *S.F. Chronicle*

Remember Sacco & Vanzetti
Remember Haymarket
Remember John Brown
Remember the slave revolts
Remember Malcolm
Remember Paracelsus
Remember Huey & Little Bobby Hutton
Remember Crazy Horse & Chief Joseph
Remember the Modoc & the Algonquin Nation
Remember Patrice Lumumba
Remember the dream of Africa
Remember Tina Modotti
Remember Makhnov & Tsvetaeva & Mayakovski
yes, goddammit, even remember Trotsky

Hey, do you remember Hypatia?
    Socrates? Giordano Bruno?
Remember my buddy, Esclarmonde de Foix
Remember Seton the Cosmopolite
Remember Edward Kelly, alchemist murdered in prison

Remember to take yr life back into yr hands
It's Memorial Day, remember
      what you love
& do it—don't wait.
Remember life hangs by a thread—
     anybody's life
& then remember the poets:
Shelley & Bob Kaufman

Remember Van Gogh & Pollock
Remember Amelia Earhart
Remember it's not a safe time & all the more reason
To do wholeheartedly what you have to do
Remember the women & men of Wounded Knee
Kent State, remember where you stand:
in the midst of empire, & the Huns
are coming.

Remember Vercingetorix, Max Jacob
Apollinaire & Suhrawardi, remember

that all you need to remember is what you love
Remember to Marry the World

REVOLUTIONARY LETTERS #94
I GUESS IT MUST BE UP TO ME
for Maude Meehan

I am in Petaluma & the war is one day old & I'm gonna read in half an hour

Thinking of you & Lucille Clifton & Audre Lorde & Adrienne Rich & my friend Maria Gillan & all us women writers—

Putting on outfits we hope look "straight" & maybe a touch of makeup

Knowing we have to tell the truth, that's the work, suspecting they'll hate it

but it's already there, in our work, on the page—

& what else cd we possibly read, with the war one day old? Not our love poems

talk about the terrorism that *is* the USA. Read for peace. . . & possibility.

Just that.

REVOLUTIONARY LETTERS #95
FOR KURT COBAIN

what we have here, USA 1994—
the freedom to self-destroy

no freedom to blaze
into complex fulfillment

REVOLUTIONARY LETTER #96
POEM AT DAWN

Empire
is its own
undoing

REVOLUTIONARY LETTER #97

WAR HAIKU,   LEBANON

even an hour of this
would be too long:
white phosphorus

great lords of the Sea!
it is Tyre that is burning—
that harbor

don't ask why I
have bad dreams
ask why if I don't

REVOLUTIONARY LETTER #98
THINGS TOO RIDICULOUS TO PUT UP WITH

Medicare with a deductible—for starters.
Are they so ambivalent
that they have to give it with one hand
take it back with the other? That's nuts!

Copayments, too.
Copayments on Medicare are like taking out sales tax
whenever you give a buck to a homeless person.
What do you think—eight and a half percent?
Ten percent? What makes sense to *you?*
Should we debate about it? Filibuster?

Income tax on social security—same thing.
Didn't I pay tax on that once
when I gave it to them to put in a fund out of which
they were supposed to give me social security?
They're not doing me a favor, it's mine—
did they think I'd forget?

Taking part of the social security on which I'm paying
income tax, and keeping it for monthly premiums
to Medicare—why do I feel
like I'm going around in a circle?

Dear Avuncular Samuel, just how many times
do you think I'll give you a piece of the same
dwindling pile of dough? Do you think I don't know
where it came from?

Here's an idea: why not take back the right
to print paper money from the Fed?
Stop paying the Federal Reserve for yr own money.

Send those old geezers from the Fed away
stick em in a retirement home with black & white TV
grade B movies, and no remote,
Just some toothpicks, and a rocking chair—
oh, and a very, VERY small ss check each month
that they never see—it goes straight to the bank. Then
let's see if they have something new to say
Something that makes more sense

This is just the beginning folks, stay tuned.
We'll be back again next week, same time
same station. And in the meantime
don't forget the Prayer:
it's the only prayer that works & I learned it
back in the '60s, from one of my kids.

All together now, let us pray:

**GOD, GOD,
DON'T MAKE EVERYTHING
RIDICULOUS**

REVOLUTIONARY LETTER #99
& ABOUT OBAMA

and if you were living
in the enemy's house
wife & kids there too

& guarded—all of you—
by known assassins

how hard wd *you* fight
do you think
for what were only—
after all—dreams

knowing there's no way
you'll actually win

what wd you be willing
—do you think—
to pay?

to see them
(those beautiful women)
walk out of there
whole
        not widowed
or orphaned

No matter what you *believed*
how much wd you
DO?

REVOLUTIONARY LETTER #100
REALITY IS NO OBSTACLE

refuse to obey
refuse to die
refuse to sleep
refuse to turn away
refuse to close your eyes
refuse to shut your ears
refuse silence when you can still sing
refuse discourse in lieu of embracement
come to no end that is not
a Beginning

REVOLUTIONARY LETTER #101

WHY MONEY MAKES ME FEEL BAD

I feel bad if I get some—why should I
have it when other folks are poor?

I feel bad if I'm broke—I'm sure
I'll end up being a burden to someone somewhere
unable to pay my half of the bills, the
rent or the mortgage.

I feel worthless & evil if I'm
behind in my taxes.   They're going
to come for me in the night   break
down my door.   I feel scared
& guilty if I get them done
on time or not I know there's a big mistake
somewhere & they'll find it
I'll go to jail.   Even tho I told the truth
have a piece of paper
to back up every number.

I feel sure my tax accountant will despise me
when he sees how little I make or
how much I owe.   He will think I am
the lowest of the low   tho I always pay him
as soon as I get the bill.

How handle this?   How feel OK?
Do I have to stop
giving money to TruthOut & other
left-wing peace-mongering animal-saving orgs?
giving so many gifts to the kids
the grand-kids, the great-grands?

Turns out I lost money last year.   My partner's
worried.   I feel guilty
cause I lost money & even more guilty
because he said "Oh dear" when I told him.
I want to crawl under the rug.

We don't have a rug, we're both
allergic to them.   I thought I'd be happy
when all the taxes were finished before deadline
but no, I'm not, I'm more miserable
than ever   even tho I owe nothing
& nothing to show for it   unless
you count this poem.

REVOLUTIONARY LETTER #102

soon the only ones
who'll know how to find us

will be Google
& those small
                    surveillance drones

REVOLUTIONARY LETTERS #103
WHERE ARE YOU?

friends know where other friends live.
not their emails or cell phone numbers
not something called their "contact information"

if she's a friend
you can show up at her door when you're in trouble.
you can mail him your new book when it's finally "out"

you can drop by when you hear they've got to move
& pack the books while they order pizza and beer
and you rent a van with yr one good credit card

she doesn't say "stay in touch" and mean Facebook
stay in touch means you touch each other, lovers or not
you crash on his floor, or bring her your old sofa
when another friend brings you his cause he's leaving town

it means when you're home from the hospital
he brings a casserole or soup for the freezer
or mops your floor, makes sure you can reach what you need

stay in touch doesn't mean a touch screen or even an iPhone
it means she'll drive you to look at the ocean
or say goodbye to your ex
he'll do yr shopping or pick up a prescription

it means one of us will stay with your three year old
if you have to stay overnight at the hospital
where you just had your 2nd baby

it means you can borrow her car; get it back to her
when everything's cleared up;   and she'll even
draw a map of the back way out of town
if you're new to this place

it means you can lay your hands along a face
that's been beautiful so long you can't even see
the edema, the death in his eyes

did you ever try to email chicken soup?
make love for the last time on Skype?
or give her that one more hug before the train leaves
by reaching all the way out thru cyber space?

REVOLUTIONARY LETTER #104

HAITI, CHILE, TIBET

LET'S STOP FOR A MOMENT TO REMEMBER WHAT WE ARE:
    a handful of tribes on a rather small rock
    where water streams over arable earth
    into larger, living waters we call "ocean"

and all is not well with our rock, it might even
                        come apart
could be it will soon be another asteroid belt
           or meteors—
               just a bunch of meteors

While our rock is shaking, and water pours from the skies
and the winds have turned demonic
could be it's time   maybe it's really time
                    to rewrite
                    the Social Contract
or at least change the rules that apply in catastrophe

Just a few suggestions:
1. ALL HANDS ON DECK
                 means just that
                 it's a *really* small planet

2. ANYONE BRINGING HELP ANYWHERE IT'S NEEDED
      BRINGING   FOOD   BLANKETS
                   WATER   MEDICINE
IS WELCOME (obviously)
don't ask where they're "from"—
      just say Thank You
      (& we'd better learn to say Thank You
      in hundreds of languages)

3. ALL BORDERS DISAPPEAR IN CATASTROPHE
      they are stupid & irrelevant anyway

4. THERE IS NO SUCH THING AS LOOTING IN A DISASTER
think about it—
after Katrina, Rita, all the storms hurricanes,
after the quakes in Chile, Haiti, Kobe, Managua—look back
                                   a bit

can you call it looting when anyone breaks plate glass
      comes out with food & water medicine
      camping supplies   whatever
is that looting or just plain sanity?
      keeping your family, keeping each other, alive

5. THERE IS NO PLACE FOR POLICE OR ARMY IN TRAGEDY
      except as facilitators
      distributors
UNARMED they should walk the streets, bringing food
      putting out fires, digging people out
      rescuing those stranded on rooftops or bridges
                       or fleeing the waters
they shd be digging latrines
      putting up shelters, helping families find each other

6. EVERY BUILDING STILL INTACT SHD OPEN ITS DOORS
to everyone
      what else are guest rooms for?
whoever comes to your door should be taken in
      I learned when I was four
she's your guest—should be given the best
      of what you've got
even if you thought she had been your enemy
Not special. It's a universal law—
      & why we're still around

7. GIVE UP CONFUSING YR PROPERTY WITH YOUR LIFE
GIVE UP CONFUSING YR PROPERTY WITH YOUR LIFE
This will save a lot of problems. Stuff comes & goes
      & holding on is like holding back a river
                 with your hands

8. STOP ASKING WHAT OTHERS "BELIEVE"
     just look in their eyes
     & see we are the same, they are the
same
     as your most beloved, be it
yr child, yr dog, yr lover

no child is hungry who is not your grandchild
HOW LONG WILL YOU LET HER WAIT?
no child is orphaned who is not your son
& WHAT WILL IT TAKE
     to make us remember our own?

REVOLUTIONARY LETTER #105

FIRE SALE—EVERYTHING MUST GO!

Well, we can't build the new society w/in the shell of the old
tho it seemed a good idea at the time
It's too late for that now.   Sorry.
I really am.   I love those old
Wobbly Songs

We can't just   **L**et the
                         State
                         Disintegrate
cause it seems it won't.   Instead it just
keeps getting stronger.   More solid.

As for those other   long-failed or failing systems
Marx has to go   & Lenin with him
Trotsky too   let's stop looking over our shoulders

No good copying Scandinavian Socialism
                                        it's just too sad
And besides   the race war
                   the class war
the skinheads   & nazis   & teabag people
will kill you   before you even try

LeftWingEcoSocioScarcityAnarchoUnionistScareYouSomehow
blahblahs

will have to go too   You all talk too much & too *long*
are too divisive   & you forget
we have to unite

     & not just build consensus

This IS *The Fire Next Time*
It's here   & it's called
Oil in the Gulf   Crack in the Ocean Floor
Earthquake in Haiti, Chile, Kobe, Managua, Tibet
It's called   Hole in the Ozone Islands Under Water

It's called The Recession Is Over, while more & more of us
     are jobless   homeless   hungry   angry   cold
     & the Market Recovers
     & the Stocks Go UP

This is The Fire Next Time's   **FIRE SALE** &
Everything Must Go

We can't fix it
by figuring out what's wrong   like a car mechanic
looking under the goddamned hood when the Car Is Totaled

we CAN
get thru this by taking a good hard look
     at what's POSSIBLE—get it?

Not what's wrong
What's possible

Not what's wrong
w/ capitalism, communism, socialism, imperialism,
                    syndicalism, unionism—you name it
But what is possible—what can be dreamed

Repeat after me: we need to look
        Not at what's wrong
        But what is possible

What wd your fantasy   your imagination say
if reality were no obstacle   which it ain't
                who wd you be?
                & what wd you do?

I don't know nothing
except that it starts   right here
don't know nothin but
            every vision is holy

so who did you say you are?
        you too
            and   you?   and   you

REVOLUTIONARY LETTER #106
EXPERIMENT

Think of it as an experiment. Tip of the tip of the
iceberg, and we ain't even on the Titanic. Not that
much "safety". But it's a start. Sit down on a curb with
somebody. Break what you got to eat in two pieces. If
they don't seem even, take the smaller piece. (It's an
experiment, you're only doing it once.) Both of you
eat what you got. Chewing slowly, noticing the taste.
Sit five to fifteen minutes together without saying
anything. Just notice how the world looks. Maybe you
feel the same as ever. Maybe not.

REVOLUTIONARY LETTER #107
THEY'RE US

they're us
    & we're starving for
    water
        for land

or air
a place to sleep

and they're our grandkids

REVOLUTIONARY LETTER #108
YET ANOTHER REV LETTER

it is the establishment—that 1%
who have given us the habit
of blame. Scapegoating. We have to
restructure our minds, shake habits
ground into our brains by TV, they are
diversion tactics, to make us forget
what we want. The resignation of a dean, a mayor
changes nothing   blaming a figurehead
brings no true change

Note: it's not scapegoating to lay blame on those
who physically harm: spray, maim, taser, shoot
their children, their mothers, their own gentle brothers—
get them off the streets if we can but remember
no dean or mayor (no governor, president) truly controls
the police force: they are mercenaries
lackeys

who see their own oppression in our faces
and try to destroy their pain by annihilating us

•

we do what we can
trusting others
will do the rest   at 78
my part is to keep going
able to walk
to witness   write what I know

•

Occupy the Planet—
that's what it's going to take
and piece by piece
it's what's got to happen.

> *Tibet has been hanging in*
> *more than half a century.*
> *This can & should*
> *be part of the discourse*
> *everywhere*

•

Occupy the Solar System.
Equal Rights for Pluto!

•

Occupy the islands
going under, the National Parks
they're closing, the beaches the forests
Occupy with hope.

•

Occupy the planet
the Oceans
as well
        as the Land

Mind is unlimited
Can go anywhere

Occupy the Night Sky,
Mother Nuit

Occupy your breath
Your Body & remember
We are one Body

Occupy with Love

REVOLUTIONARY LETTER #109
FOR ANNIE BANKS

choose
          yr battles
"pick yr shots"

you have only
              so much
ammunition—

                where
will it do
          the most

damage?

REVOLUTIONARY LETTER #110

FOR AMIRI BARAKA

don' matter was it
yr left foot went bad
or yr right

don' matter yr lungs
or yr heart

don' matter if that
mass
          on yr liver was
malignant

or what's been wrong
so long
          w/ yr kidneys

don't matter
                    herbs
western medicine
                    acupuncture

or why you didn't
go
    to those appointments

don't matter how much you drank
or *if* you drank

don't matter you did or you didn't
take drugs

        meaning **meds**
take drugs

        meaning **drugs**

what matters when all of us
      what we wrote
           what we thought
is lost

    (& don't kid yourself,
    Ginsberg
    it's all of it
    gonna be lost)

what matters:
        every place
        you read

        every line
        you wrote

every dog-eared book
        or pamphlet
on somebody's shelf

every skinny hopeful kid
you grinned that grin at

while they said
> *they thought they could write*
> *they thought they could fight*
they knew for sure
> *they could change the world*

every human dream
you heard
      or inspired

after the book-signing
after the reading
             after one more
             unspeakable
             faculty dinner

What matters:
        the memory
of the poem
        taking root in
thousands
      of minds . . .

REVOLUTIONARY LETTER #111
DON'T TURN AWAY

if you are working on something now don't turn away &
especially if it hurts don't look away how many how deep
the sore flesh eaten to bone by infection don't look away
like hyena Vulture waiting guardians   don't look away
guardians of the edge, of Port-au-Prince, don't look don't
look away the wraiths of forbidden hope don't   forbidden
love don't   dust whose skulls we bury who   and bury
where   shall we keep the dead don't look away don't blink
don't turn   it is the same north for the old ones don't look
away   south for the children I thought they came to stay
look now look thru yr tears if you have any if there are
any tears left   look they magnify tears magnify what you
can still see
what   what   look

                    do you know mud warm mud what
breeds in it no don't look it up don't study it's all before
your eyes it's in your skin your memory you can taste it
too don't refuse your memories they ARE you   don't look
away don't let that one lie face down any longer turn it
over is it he or she IS there a face part of a face look closer
eyeballs are delicious to many zero in   don't go   we have
only just come to this place it's not a horror show.
                              what does it
mean to rot? a great healer asked he looked he invited all to
look. what does   it mean to ROT   what comes apart in
the moist air   look in the rain   look in the streaming mud

what is a mass grave? this is not a rhetorical question.   stand on the brink & look look close as you can never mind the smell this will only take a moment I promise   how long do you actually think you have?   stand on the edge the brink   who is rotting here?   what falls to pieces?   how do you know a piece?

look in   discover stumble by accident on a grave at the edge of town   is it fresh? look closer is it fairly new? the mud is alive with forms moving shaping self-destructing recombinant they are not fearful any longer look bear witness look   earth is mass grave in the warming air

REVOLUTIONARY LETTER #112

Queen showed us how

sing We are the champions of the world

While the ground under your feet is burning

Sing into the mic

Don't hide your burning hair

Look proud   stride off

When your microphone catches fire.

REVOLUTIONARY LETTER #113

Dream after Christchurch

The prophet decrees all that died return

and glistening with marvelous help

Walk into

Dark Futures.

REVOLUTIONARY LETTER #114

ANTHEM
for Bruce Conner

Them Lords, them Lords
They're gonna provide!
Whoever they are
They're on everybody's side!
Them gods and goddesses
Under the sea
They're baking cookies
For you & me!

We'll walk in the thunderstorm
& never get wet!
Just how we're gonna do it
Is anybody's bet.
'Cause tomorrow isn't
Just another day
It's a way to make yesterday
Go away!

Destiny, Necessity
They're all on our side
So come on, join the
Existentialist sleigh ride.
And shout "**Das Vedanya!**"
And "Yippee-eye-ay!"
Till famine plague and war
Have melted away.

I think you get the picture
Nobody's boss!
So pull on your pants
& get on yr horse.
Or sit on a chair or cushion
with an "**OM!**" and a shout
While Container and Contained
Turn inside out!!

GOODBYE NKRUMAH

And yet, where would we be without the American culture
Bye bye blackbird, as Miles plays it, in the '50s
Those coffee malteds?
When the radio told me there was dancing in the streets,
I knew we had engineered another coup;
Bought off another army. And I wondered
what the guys at the Black Arts Theatre were saying
and sent them my love, and my help, which they would not

accept

Why should they? It's their war, all I can do is wait
Is not put detergents in the washingmachine, so the soil will still

be productive

when the black men, or the Chinese, come to cultivate it.

I remember a news photo of you stepping off a plane somewhere,
so cool, so straight a look, and so black.
There was nothing we could do but do you in.
You understand, of course. There is nothing we can do

but shoot students
buy armies
like the British before us killing the Zulus—
now they are fat and placid
their country a shambles.
Well, for us it won't end like that
not quite so simply:

when the Nevele Country Club, the Hotel Americana
when Beverly Hills and the Cliff House
come crashing down, it will be Shiva who dances,
the sky behind him orange (saffron) a great black mushroom
painted on it somewhere
(it was a mushroom killed Buddha)
will kill him again, compassion has to go

a few of us tried it, we tried to stop it with printing
we tried to protect you with mimeograph machines
green posters LUMUMBA LIVES flooded Harlem in those days
well, the best thing to do with a mimeograph is to drop it
from a five story window, on the head of a cop

we buy the arms and the armed men, we have placed them
on all the thrones of South America
we are burning the jungles, the beasts will rise up against us
even now those small jungle people with black eyes
look calmly at us out of their photographs
and it is their calm that will finish us, it is the calm
of the earth itself.

March 1966

TO THE UNNAMED BUDDHIST NUN, WHO BURNED HERSELF TO DEATH ON THE NIGHT OF JUNE 3, 1966

Outside your temple wall. Stone or wood, I can't
quite see the detail; under this last full moon
which I did see. Moon of this June, unearthly light
heavy with potency, the air filled with the smells
and buzzing of springtime

you with your shaved head and can
of kerosene. Under what driving form
of ecstasy? I pray to taste it once

your soaked robe chilly in the spring night wind

> *"Oh nun, is it hot in there?"*
> *"Only a stupid person like yourself would ask*
> *such a question."*

RANT, FROM A COOL PLACE

*"I see no end of it, but the turning upside down
of the entire world."*—Erasmus

We are in the middle of a bloody, heartrending revolution
Called America, called the Protestant reformation, called
        Western man,
Called individual consciousness, meaning I need a refrigerator
        and a car
And milk and meat for the kids so I can discover that I don't
        need a car
Or a refrigerator, or meat, or even milk, just rice and a place with
        no wind to sleep next to someone
Two someones keeping warm in the winter learning to weave
To pot and to putter, learning to steal honey from bees, wearing
        the bedclothes by day, sleeping under
(or in) them at night; hoarding bits of glass, colored stones,
        and stringing beads
How long before we come to that blessed definable state
Known as buddhahood, primitive man, people in a landscape
together like trees, the second childhood of man

I don't know if I will make it somehow nearer by saying all this
out loud, for christs sake, that Stevenson was killed, that
        Shastri was killed
both having dined with Marietta Tree
the wife of a higher-up in the CIA
both out of their own countries mysteriously dead, as how
        many others

as Marilyn Monroe, wept over in so many tabloids
done in for sleeping with Jack Kennedy—this isn't a poem—
                full of cold prosaic fact
thirteen done in in the Oswald plot: Jack Ruby's cancer that
                disappeared in autopsy
the last of a long line—and they're waiting to get Tim Leary
Bob Dylan
Allen Ginsberg
LeRoi Jones—as, who killed Malcolm X? They give themselves
                away
with TV programs on the Third Reich, and I wonder if I'll live
                to sit in Peking or Hanoi
see TV programs of LBJ's Reich: our great ss analyzed, our
                money exposed, the plot to keep Africa
genocide in Southeast Asia now in progress Laos Vietnam
                Thailand Cambodia O soft-spoken Sukarno
O great stone Buddhas with sad negroid lips torn down by us by
                the red guard all one force
one leveling mad mechanism, grinding it down to earth and
                swamp to sea to powder
till Mozart is something a few men can whistle
or play on a homemade flute and we bow to each other
telling old tales half remembered gathering shells
learning again "all beings are from the very beginning Buddhas"
or glowing and dying radiation and plague we come to that final
                great love illumination
"FROM THE VERY FIRST NOTHING IS."

January 1967

NEW MEXICO POEM

I—NEW MEXICO

Even the sunsets here haven't won me over
Haven't convinced me
Simply, this *isn't* to me familiar land
Pink ears of jackrabbits high among the sagebrush
Don't tell me any different

I suppose we all learn; there is in Herodotus
the tale of Greek soldiers settling near Thebes
each given a woman and land, one woman
so like another, one field . . .
But they at least moved from glitter into gold:
As we step backwards even the clay becomes coarser
my thoughts echo big against the high, flat valley
they roll back, bigger than life, to devour my dreams

II—CORN DANCE, TAOS PUEBLO

Red people in blankets wait for returning woodchucks.
(I know it, though they don't say it)
and beavers
and chipmunks, and possums, and otters, gophers, white people
poison the prairie dogs, if a dog find a dead one & eat it
he dies—what kind of game
is that?

Red people in blankets stand on their high flat roofs
outlined against the sky
they chant—they sing and pray and it could be
Morocco except the houses aren't white
the women sell jewelry, giggling, the little boys
catch fish with their bare hands, in the sacred river

III—THE JOURNEY

The city I want to visit is made of porcelain
The dead are gathered there, they are at their best:
Bob Thompson
in his checkered jacket & little hat, his grin
full of cocaine, spinning down the street; Frank drunk
spitting out tales of Roussel, of Mayakovsky
brief anecdotes over bacon and eggs on a roll,
his keenness against the wind; Freddie in pointed shoes
drinking an egg cream, his leotard over his shoulder
in a little bag, waving amphetamine hands at the sky

The porcelain city glitters, I feel my friends
hastening to join it & to join me there:
Bob Creeley tearing through Buffalo streets seeking entry
John Wieners holding still, mumbling and waiting
tears under his eyelids; I walk in that brittle city
still sleepy and arrogant and desperately in love . . .

IV—EVENING, TAOS VALLEY

How did we come here? my bones
keep asking me.
They see themselves lying bleached on the sand floor of the valley
they don't like it
don't like it at all

the moon like a bleached skull
sits behind an abandoned house
the house is melting, it is becoming
part of the field

Which ones are weeds? the garden
teeters on the edge of success
We live in a mud cave, with a stone floor
a rather luxurious cave, with running water.

V—FAREWELL, NEW MEXICO

One thing they never mention in Western movies or those
     ballads they're always writing about wide open spaces:
Sagebrush has a smell
And there are hills, distinctly flesh-colored, lying down
in front of the purple ones.
O wondrous wide open spaces!
O dust on the roads!
O Rio Grande Gorge!
Green Taos Valley full of thunderstorms and mosquitoes
Mountain with two peaks, sacred to Taos indians
Great ceremonial lake, fought over in congress
O Taos indians, with your braids wrapped in leather
may you keep your sacred lake and whatever else
you would like to keep
may you drink with brother buffalo on its edge
when no one at all remembers the US Congress

As for me I have just changed from the D to the A train
in a dark tunnel you Indians wouldn't believe;
a metal tube is shrieking as it carries me to an island
with four million people on it, eating supper.
The newspaper tells me that there is a war in Newark.
My hope is small but constant: black men shall tear down
                              the thing they cannot name.
They will make room again for the great sea birds
the woods
will spring up thicker than even you remember

Where you are, it is two hours earlier
the breeze is cold, the sun is very hot
the horses are standing around, wishing for trees
It is possible I shall see you dance again
on your hills, in your beads, if the gods are very kind

DEE'S SONG

Velvet lady, lay on velvet pillows
    in a house where the rain came in
Eucalyptus trees outside the velvet windows
    long silver fingers talking in the wind
Her eyes on the TV, her hair on a pillow
    horse in her arm, making gold
The lady was smiling, her thoughts ebbed and billowed
    her smokedreams were tapestry old

        The wooden house stood in a madrone grove
        Inside it were mirrors of glass
        And candlestick niches, and storybook dishes
        And vases of pewter and brass

California lady, slim and stylish as a leopard
    her tie-dye velvets lying on a shelf
Walking to her mailbox, airy hearted as a shepherd-
    ess to find the smack she shoots into herself
Old man's gone south again in search of bread and glory powder
    eating percodan in all that canyon sun
The lady wears blue rhinestones and her magic doesn't founder:
    target practice with a tin can and a gun

        The wooden house stood in a madrone grove
        Inside it were mirrors of glass
        And candlestick niches, and storybook dishes
        And vases of pewter and brass

Iridescent lady talking horoscopes and witches
    cooking oatmeal porridge in the morning cold
Reading dirty tarot cards and washing painted dishes
    while the ferns at your door fall to mold
And mushrooms are growing as big as your fist
    and the skyscrapers teeter and sway
And the wraiths in your woodswamp all tell you to cool it
    but then, that was never your way

        O lady I hope you have ice in your heart
        And the steel in your eyes is at rest
        They've locked you away for five years and a day
        For the judge and the jury know best

There's dust on your candles, and wind in your bedroom
    eats perfume you used in your hair
Your filched Goodwill wardrobe is scattered thru crash pads
    where younger girls look for their share
You longed for a baby, a green-eyed madonna
    whose swaddling clothes bundle the night
The stars drew your circle, like marshlights they mock you
    my sister in a cage, sleep tight

May 1968

CANTICLE OF ST. JOAN
for Robert Duncan

1.
It is in God's hands. How can I *decide*
France shall be free? And yet, with the clear song
of thrush, of starling, comes the word, decide
For human agency is freely chosen. I embrace
the iron crown, the nettle shirt, as I
embraced our lord god in the darkling wood
He of the silver hooves and flashing mane
Who shall be nameless.
Nameless as spruce and holly, which endure.
Holy St. Michael, but the ace of swords
is bitter! And the grail
not to be drunk, but carried into shelter.
The dragon, my naga, purrs, it lays its claws
about the bars which will soon close around me.
I stand in its breath, that fire, and read love
in its eyes like crystal balls which mirror gore
of the burning, pillaged cities I set free.
O brew me mistletoe, unveil the well
I shall lie down again with him who must be nameless
and sink my strong teeth into unhuman flesh.

2.
Blessed be the holy saints, now and forever.
Blessed be Margaret & Bridget
Blessed be spruce & fir.
The sacred waterfall, Diana's bath, the wind
which brings iron clouds.
They fly out of the sea to the north, they recommend
that I wear woman's dress, they do not see
that I am Luci-fer, light bearer, lead & I follow
Mother, Sara-la-Kali, sacred Diana, I could have borne
a babe to our sovereign god but would not
in this captivity, this blood
on my hands and no other
BUT SAINT GEORGE I WILL CONQUER
dragonslayer
who seeks to destroy the light in this holy forest
the yellow men call Europe

3.
Where is my helmet? Battle
is what I crave, shock of lance, death cry, the air
filled with the jostling spirits of the dead,
meat & drink, the earth enriched with brain & entrail
horses' hooves sliding, the newly fallen
finding soft soggy bed on the fallen leaves, tears are too light
for this, GRAIL IS BLOOD IS HOLLY
red with our sorrow as we reclaim the ground
free to lie again with the horned man, the overlords
must build their edifices elsewhere, here we stomp
in our wooden shoes on the bare earth, take in our arms
boughs of the great trees, the misty fabrics of wee folk
flesh of our brethren soon to grow cold, the children
half imp who live on earth as it were hell, I hear
the Voice, it bids me seek no forgiveness for none
is my share, my blessing is leaden sky, the sacred blood
of the children of forest shines like jewels
upon it.

4.
O am I salamander, do I dance or leap
with pain, can I indeed fall & falling
fall out of this fire? half charred to smolder
black under blackening sky, the god is good
who made the stake strong, made the chains strong, I laugh
I think I laugh I hear peals of unholy laughter
like bells. The cross was ours before you holy men, its secret
there, where the two sticks meet, you cannot fathom.
I hear the cart creak home that brought me, the driver
won't even stay for this end—leap, pirouette.
Inside the grail is fire, the deep draught
melted rubies, blood of the most high god
whose name is Satan, and whose planet earth
I reclaim for the Bundschuh, sons of men.
My hair is burning and the mist is blue
which cracks my brain, I am not in the flame, I am the flame
the sun pours down, the Voice is a mighty roar
O little children's bones! the sword & cup
are shivered into stars.

Books by Diane di Prima

Publication History

The original mimeograph edition of *Revolutionary Letters* was published in 1968 by the Diggers' press, Communications Co. in San Francisco. Subsequent 1968 editions were produced by the Poetry Project at St. Mark's Church in New York City and the Artists Workshop Press in Ann Arbor. Another edition was produced in 1969 in London by Long Hair Books.

Between 1971 and 1979, City Lights Books published four editions of *Revolutionary Letters* as Number Twenty-Seven in the Pocket Poets Series, each time expanded with new poems. In 2007, another expanded edition was published by Last Gasp in San Francisco.

The present City Lights edition, published on the occasion of the 50th anniversary of the original and returning the book to the Pocket Poets Series, is again expanded and includes 21 additional poems.

This 50th anniversary edition was prepared under the direction of Diane di Prima.

Index